Rachel's
Everyday
Kitchen

Simple, delicious family food

HarperCollins*Publishers*

CONTENTS

INTRODUCTION

WE ALL LEAD SUCH HECTIC LIVES, and as a busy working parent I understand how challenging it can be to cook wholesome food for your family every day. During my many years as a cookery teacher I have tried and tested family friendly, hassle-free recipes on my children so that you too can easily cook for your family without ever compromising on flavour.

Cooking for yourself and for your family is such an important thing to be able to do. Eating good food has a profound impact on your health, energy and outlook. It may take a little longer than heating up a ready-meal or ordering a take-away, but it is the only way of ensuring you know where all the ingredients come from. Cooking ensures your family's meals are nutritious and delicious but can also be creative and fun!

In this book, I hope to show you how to make the most of your time in the kitchen and how to make best use of the ingredients that you buy. With a bit of forward thinking, you can turn one meal into several different dishes, keeping waste to a minimum. If you're going to buy the best ingredients you can afford, then it's vital that nothing is wasted. Cooked potatoes left over from lunch could be made into a delicious and comforting tartiflette for supper on another day, for instance, while roasted butternut squash enjoyed hot at the table could be transformed into a tasty salad for a packed lunch.

Buying fresh ingredients that are in season –
asparagus and rhubarb in the spring, for instance,
or plums and squash in the autumn – will ensure you're
getting maximum value and flavour from what you eat.
Cooking in bulk can save both time and money, too.
As you'll see, I've included lots of recipes that are just
as easy to make in a slightly larger quantity and then
freeze the extra portion. Stews, soups, pies, along with
many other recipes, can all be doubled up and frozen
for another day. So rather than resorting to a ready
meal, you can defrost something homemade instead –
guaranteed to be more nutritious and much tastier!

Just a few small adjustments to your weekly routine
could reap big rewards for you and your family, with
delicious, healthy meals and more time spent together
enjoying them. With its straightforward recipes and lots
of practical, thrifty tips, I hope this book will go some
way to achieving just that.

MEAL PLANNING

Menu planning for the week is really worth doing if you're a busy person, particularly if you have a family to feed.

If you have time to spare on a Monday, for instance, then how about making a ragù sauce (see page 130) to eat that evening with pasta, knowing that you'll have enough left over to serve with enchiladas for supper later in the week? Equally, Sunday's leftover roast chicken (see page 82) could be turned into Quick Chicken Casserole (see page 86) on Tuesday, when you know you'll be home late and will appreciate an almost-ready meal. The roast chicken carcass, of course, will make a wonderfully nutritious (and virtually free) stock, which can be used in a myriad different recipes, including many in this book. It's really satisfying, as well as hugely important, to use up every morsel that might otherwise get thrown away.

That said, having a very specific plan for your meals isn't always realistic. It's easy to find yourself out shopping without a list – either because you've forgotten it or because you didn't have time to write it in the first place! That's why it's so important to have a really well-stocked store cupboard, fridge and freezer. Then, when you find yourself 'listless' when out shopping, you can buy a bit of meat or a few fresh vegetables in the knowledge that you have enough at home to make a full meal out of them.

Even though the price of food seems to be going up all the time, you don't need to spend lots of money to produce delicious, nutritious meals. You can still be thrifty without compromising on quality or having to settle for inferior produce. One of the best ways to save money is to buy cheaper cuts of meat, usually the less popular parts of an animal. They may require a little more care in the kitchen – long slow cooking, for example – but can result in better-tasting dishes than ones made using more expensive cuts. Pork belly (see page 160), for instance, is one of my favourite cuts of pork, moist and wonderfully rich. Lamb's neck (see page 145) is very affordable, too, and makes for a fabulous-tasting dish.

The same applies to eating fish that are less popular, such as whiting, pollock and ling. Used fresh, these types of fish are often just as good as cod or haddock and work so well in the Fish Gratin with Crunchy, Cheesy Breadcrumbs (see page 66) or Sunshine Fish Curry (see page 57).

Vegetables are almost always cheaper than meat, so a vegetarian meal is usually more affordable while still packed with flavour, especially if the vegetables are roasted, as in the Roasted Butternut Squash with Thyme (see page 213), or enhanced with spices, as in the Moroccan Chickpea Tagine (see page 182). You can save money on vegetables, too; by buying local produce that is in season, you'll not only be eating it at its most delicious, but not paying for all those road or air miles included in the price of vegetables from further afield.

Then there are leftovers, of course, which you can simply reuse cold, reheat or use as an ingredient in a completely new dish. Mashed potato, for instance, is endlessly versatile and can be used as a pie topping or as the basis for Bubble and Squeak (see page 200) or Instant Cullen Skink (see page 64).

COOKING AHEAD AND IN BATCHES

Cooking will always take a little time, if perhaps not as much as you think, but there are many ways of saving time in the kitchen or prepping ahead so you don't have to watch over a dish from the beginning to the end of cooking it. Throughout the recipes you'll find tips to help you with this.

Numerous dishes, including many recipes in this book, can be prepared ahead to different stages. The bread doughs can be left to prove in the fridge overnight, for instance, to slow down the process, enabling you start making a loaf one day and bake it fresh the next. A number of recipes can also be prepared up to the point of cooking them and then stored in the fridge or even the freezer, so all you need to do is bake them for a wonderful freshly cooked meal. The Chicken and Ham Pie (see page 89), Cheesy Kale Bake (see page 207) and Classic Lasagne (see page 133) are just a few of the dishes that can be made ahead in this way.

It isn't just one-pot dishes that can be made ahead. While none of the recipes in this book are particularly complicated, if I'm making a dish with a number of different components I will usually make part of it ahead. It's rare for me to spend more than an hour in the kitchen without some distraction or other! Hence, for example, in the Smoked Mackerel Tart (see page 58) or Cheese, Tomato and Basil Tart (see page 120), I might blind-bake the tart case several hours

ahead of time, so that finishing it is only a matter of making a simple filling and baking in the oven. In the meatball recipes (see pages 128 and 137), the meatballs themselves can be made ahead and kept in the fridge or freezer, so that completing the recipe another time takes only minutes.

Another great way of saving time is cooking food in batches and storing these in the fridge or freezer. Pasta sauces are perfect candidates for this. The sauce for the Tagliatelle al Ragù (see page 130) or for the Sausage Pasta Pot (see page 167) can easily be made in double quantities and the extra portion stored in the freezer. Some soups are ideal for this treatment, such as the Red Lentil Soup (see page 194) or the Thai Butternut Squash Soup (see page 215), while others, such as the Minestrone (see page 174), are best eaten fresh and won't keep so well.

While you can often save time and prep recipes ahead, you'll still have to do that prep at some point! And the best thing here, short of training as a chef, is to invest in a nice big chopping board, if you don't already have one, and a good-quality knife that is properly sharp!

STORING AND FREEZING

The organised cook will save time and money by becoming good friends with their fridge and freezer. The freezer is especially useful if you're planning ahead as certain foods can be frozen for up to three months.

Meat and fish will freeze well. The texture won't be exactly the same when thawed, but if frozen and defrosted properly it will be almost as good. Stock freezes perfectly, as do certain sauces, soups (see opposite) and bread. When freezing bread, it's quite a good idea to slice the loaf first (unless you'd prefer to keep it whole, of course), then store in the freezer in an airtight container or sealed bag. That way you can just take a few slices out of the freezer at a time.

All food in the freezer should be kept well wrapped or in airtight containers. There's a reason why Tupperware parties were once so popular – good-quality containers in varying sizes are incredibly useful! I'll often divide a large batch of soup or stew between a few smaller-sized containers, so a great-tasting and nutritious meal is only a matter of defrosting and reheating.

Whether you're using the fridge or freezer, it's important to label things carefully, noting what they are and the date they've been stored. I know full well the tragedy of finding something hidden away unlabelled at the back of the freezer and not having a clue what it is or for how long its been frozen. When freezing meat or fish it's especially important to ensure the wrapping or container is clearly labelled with the date.

In most instances, you need to leave food out to defrost over a few hours before reheating it. Soups or stews are useful if you are in a hurry as you can just place them in a pan on the stove and gently warm them over a low heat without 're-cooking' them. Meals that have been frozen uncooked, such as the Classic Lasagne (see page 133) or the Smoked Haddock Pie (see page 63), should be defrosted fully before cooking, otherwise the centre will stay cold and not cook through properly.

ONE MEAL TURNED INTO MANY

All sorts of meals can be turned into many with just a little imagination. Leftovers needn't be thrown away, but can become a delicious base for your next meal. Creating these frugal feasts is a smart and satisfying way to make the most of good-quality ingredients.

Leftover roast chicken is a particularly useful ingredient. Roast a chicken on a Sunday and the nutrient-rich carcass and any leftover meat can be transformed into four easy family meals for the week ahead. The carcass can be used to make a stock with vegetables you'll have lurking in your vegetable drawer. Then you have an instant soup base, a broth for a quick storecupboard noodle supper or a base for luxurious risotto. You can use the leftover meat in a salad the next day or in a substantial supper such as the Quick Chicken Casserole or Chicken and Ham Pie. So many dishes in this book give you more than one meal. Look for ⬛ symbol for other leftovers ideas.

Clockwise from top left: CHICKEN AND HAM PIE *(p89),* CHICKEN STOCK *(p19),* RED LENTIL SOUP, made from stock *(p194),* QUICK CHICKEN CASSEROLE *(p86)*

LUNCHBOX IDEAS

I love having a small packed lunch with me when I'm out and know I might have to eat on the go. Even it's just a salad or a slice of something, I find it reassuring to know I've got a tasty homemade snack with me if I'm out and about. Packed lunches are absolutely not just for children! They're an excellent way of saving money as well as ensuring you've tucking into something nutritious and full of flavour, whether you're in the office or simply out and about.

Sandwiches work well, of course, the bread providing a nice neat 'package'. Both the Pork Sliders with Red Cabbage Salad (see page 163) and the Pulled Lamb Toasted Baps (see page 154) would make fabulous lunches, especially as they use meat left over from a previous meal. You could also try wraps – the Steak Fajitas (see page 138) would make a divine packed lunch.

A salad would also be excellent for a lunchbox, filling the container nicely as well as being healthy for you. Salad leaves, though, won't do well if dressed and kept trapped in a lunchbox for hours. If you're taking a green salad, then make sure to store the dressing separately and dress the leaves just before eating. Non-leaf salads would be fine, of course. The Nutty Quinoa Salad (see page 185) is both super-healthy and sustaining, as is the Bulgur Wheat Salad (see page 90), with or without the chicken. Other lunchbox favourites of mine are the Pickled Beetroot, Sweet Potato and Lentil Salad (see page 193) and Roasted Butternut Squash Salad (see page 219), not to mention the Chicken, Fennel and Orange Salad (see page 98) and Broccoli Orzo Salad (see page 204).

A slice or two of leftover tart are ideal for a packed lunch. Try the Smoked Mackerel Tart (see page 58), Cheese, Tomato and Basil Tart (see page 120) or the Potato, Smoked Salmon and Dill Tart (see page 54). The Spinach, Bacon and Gruyère Frittata (see page 116) would be delicious too, an essential lunchbox item for any Spaniard.

Clockwise from top left: PICKLED BEETROOT, SWEET POTATO AND LENTIL SALAD *(p193)*, PULLED LAMB TOASTED BAPS *(p150)*, PIZZAS *(p32–37)*, NUTTY QUINOA SALAD *(p185)*

STOCKS

NO STOCK CUBE, however handy or however good the brand, can compare with a homemade broth of boiled bones, vegetables and herbs. The recipes on the following pages are just a guideline; you can add to the stockpot most meat and vegetables that you have to spare or scraps you might otherwise throw away.

Making stock is a good way to use up leek or fennel tops, for instance, a mushroom or two, or some leftover sprigs of herbs, even the peelings from a piece of root ginger. Try not to add too much of any one vegetable, however, or the flavour may dominate the stock. And avoid starchy vegetables such as potatoes or parsnips as they will simply disintegrate and make the stock cloudy. By way of meat, livers are unwelcome as they will make the stock bitter, but necks, hearts and wing tips are perfect for adding to the pot.

STOCK TIPS

To see if the stock is cooked enough, taste a little scrap of meat on the bones and if it still has a bit of flavour then it means the stock needs to be cooked for longer. When fully cooked, all the flavour from the meat and bones (and vegetables) will have transferred to the broth.

––––––––

If you wish to concentrate the flavour, then place the stock (after cooling it and removing the fat) on a high heat and boil, uncovered, to reduce the liquid. If you reduce it to about quarter of its original volume (it should taste quite meaty), you could, once the liquid has cooled, pour it into ice-cube trays, then freeze, giving you your own frozen stock cubes.

––––––––

Once made, stock will keep in the fridge for up to three days. It can be kept in the freezer – poured into several smaller containers or an ice-cube tray – for up to three months.

CHICKEN STOCK

Makes 1–2 litres (1¾–3½ pints)

1 chicken carcass, cooked or raw, and any
　leftover bones

1–2 carrots, peeled and halved lengthways

1 onion, peeled and halved, or 4 spring
　onions, halved

1 leek (or just the green part)

1 stick of celery

Bunch of parsley stalks

1 sprig of thyme

Small bay leaf

Place all the ingredients in a large saucepan and fill the pan with enough water to cover the carcass and vegetables by about 8cm (3in). Bring to the boil, then reduce the heat and simmer for 2–3 hours, skimming away any foam that rises to the surface. Cook until you have a well-flavoured stock (see tip on page 18).

Strain the stock so that you are left with just the liquid. Discard the vegetables and carcass and allow to cool before chilling further in the fridge. As it cools the fat will solidify and rise to the surface, enabling it to be lifted off easily and discarded.

⊘ **Vegetable stock:** Prepare and cook as above, simply omitting the chicken carcass and bones.

DUCK STOCK

I find duck stock really benefits from using a carcass or bones that have been roasted first. It gives it a sweeter, more intense flavour. If I'm making the stock for an Asian recipe, I always add slices of root ginger to the pot, but if it's for something like a potato and thyme soup I'll often leave it out.

Makes 1–2 litres (1¾–3½ pints)
1 duck carcass, cooked or raw, and any leftover bones
1 onion, peeled and halved
1 carrot, peeled and halved lengthways
2 unpeeled cloves of garlic, bashed
A few parsley or coriander stalks
Good pinch of salt
2 slices of unpeeled root ginger (optional)

If roasting the duck carcass and bones, place in a roasting tin and cook in the oven (preheated to 200°C/400°F/Gas mark 6) for 20–30 minutes or until browned.

Place the carcass and bones in a large saucepan and add the remaining ingredients. Fill the pan with enough water to cover the carcass and vegetables by about 8cm (3in). Bring to the boil, then reduce the heat and simmer for 2–3 hours, skimming away any foam that rises to the surface. Cook until you have a well-flavoured stock (see tip on page 18).

Strain the stock, discarding the bones and other ingredients, then allow to cool before placing in the fridge to chill further. As the liquid cools, the fat will set and rise to the top, making it easy to lift off and save to use another time, such as for roasting potatoes.

BEEF STOCK

Makes 2–3 litres (3½–5 pints)
2kg (4lb 4oz) raw beef bones (with some meat left on)
2 onions, peeled and halved
2 carrots, peeled and halved
2 sticks of celery
Bunch of parsley stalks
1 sprig of rosemary
1 sprig of thyme
Bay leaf

Preheat the oven to 230°C (450°F), Gas mark 8.

Place the bones in a roasting tin and roast in the oven for about 30 minutes or until browned.

Transfer the roasted bones to a large saucepan with the rest of the ingredients and fill the pan with enough water to cover the bones and vegetables by about 8cm (3in). Bring to the boil, then reduce the heat and simmer gently for 5–6 hours, skimming away any foam that rises to the surface. Cook until you have a well-flavoured stock (see tip on page 18).

Strain the stock, discarding the bones and vegetables, and allow to cool before transferring to the fridge to chill further. The fat will rise to the top of the liquid as it cools, making it is easy to skim off.

NOTES ON INGREDIENTS

- All the eggs used in the recipes are large.

- Fruit and vegetables are medium-sized unless otherwise stated.

- Where a specific kind of sugar isn't mentioned in a recipe, use caster or granulated.

- Although the type of olive oil isn't specified in the recipes and you can use whatever you have to hand, I always use extra-virgin olive oil as I think it is better for you and has the best flavour. Even if it's a little more expensive, it's absolutely worth it in my view.

- I always use whole milk as I love its creamy richness, however, if you like you can use semi-skimmed for cooking. Avoid using skimmed milk as it just doesn't have the same richness, particularly in baking recipes.

Oven temperatures
The oven temperatures in this book are for a conventional oven, but if I am using a fan oven, then I reduce the temperature by 10 per cent.

SYMBOLS

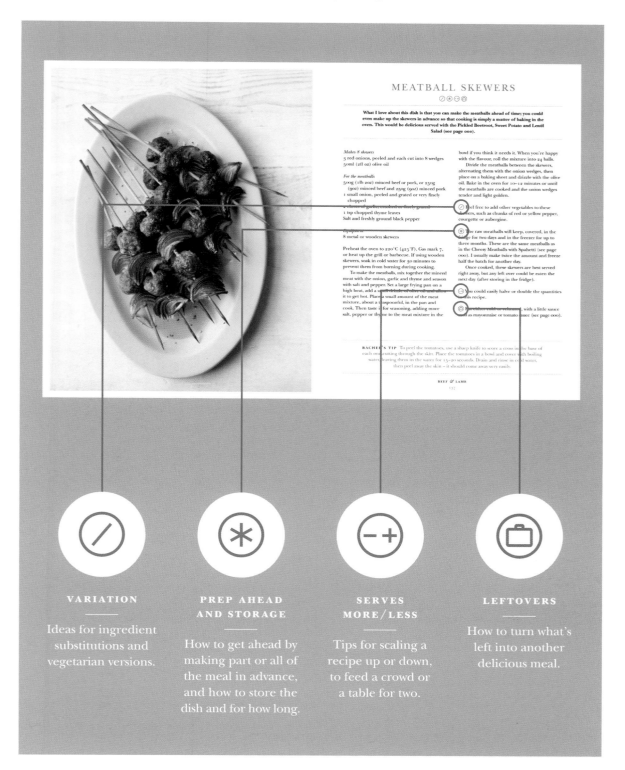

VARIATION

Ideas for ingredient substitutions and vegetarian versions.

PREP AHEAD AND STORAGE

How to get ahead by making part or all of the meal in advance, and how to store the dish and for how long.

SERVES MORE/LESS

Tips for scaling a recipe up or down, to feed a crowd or a table for two.

LEFTOVERS

How to turn what's left into another delicious meal.

PIZZA & BREAD

MAKING BREAD ISN'T DIFFICULT but you do need to allow time for the dough to double in size – plus a bowl big enough to accommodate this, of course. The time the dough takes to rise can depend on a number of different factors: the amount of yeast used, and whether it's fresh or dried; the temperature of the water; the type of flour being used; and the amount of moisture in the dough. Depending on these factors, the dough can take 1–2 hours (or even up to 3 hours on a cold day) to double in size in the first instance and 20–45 minutes for the second rising or 'proving' (when the dough is shaped). On the other hand, you may prefer to actually slow down the process to give you more flexibility about when to bake the bread. If so, you could use cold instead of warm water to mix with the yeast and place the dough in the fridge instead of putting it in a warm place to rise. After the dough has been kneaded, placed in the bowl and covered in cling film, it can be left in the fridge where it will take 16–24 hours to double in size. When the dough has been shaped, it can be placed in the fridge again, where it will take about 6 hours to rise.

FLATBREADS WITH A SPICED CANNELLINI BEAN DIP

✳ ⊝ ▱

Flatbreads are eaten across the Middle East and much of Africa. They make a lovely alternative to crusty bread, chewier and often flavoured with spices and nuts. I like to serve them with a dip such as this one or as part of a main meal, with the Lamb Kofta Tagine (see page 142), for instance, or the Spicy Spatchcock Chicken (see page 100).

Makes 8 flatbreads
For the flatbreads
225ml (8fl oz) warm water
1 tsp caster sugar
1½ tsp dried yeast or 15g (½oz) fresh yeast or
   1 x 7g sachet of fast-action yeast
375g (13oz) strong white flour, plus extra for dusting
1 tsp salt
1 tbsp coriander seeds, toasted and ground
   (see tip below)
1 tbsp cumin seeds, toasted and ground
   (see tip below)
50g (2oz) shelled pistachios, chopped
1 tbsp olive oil, plus extra for greasing

For the spiced cannellini bean dip
2 x 400g tins of cannellini beans, drained and
   rinsed, or 250g (9oz) dried cannellini beans,
   soaked overnight and cooked (see tip below)
1 tsp coriander seeds, toasted and ground
   (see tip below)
1 tsp cumin seeds, toasted and ground
   (see tip below)

3 cloves of garlic, peeled and crushed
   or finely grated
2 tbsp chopped parsley, plus extra to garnish
50ml (2fl oz) olive oil, plus extra for drizzling
Salt and freshly ground black pepper

In a measuring jug, mix together the warm water, sugar and yeast and leave to stand in a warm place for 5 minutes or until the mixture becomes creamy. If using fast-action yeast, there's no need to let the mixture stand.

Sift the flour, salt and spices into a large bowl, or the bowl of an electric food mixer fitted with a dough hook, and mix in the nuts. Add the olive oil to the yeast mixture, then pour this into the dry ingredients and bring together to form a dough.

If making by hand, tip the dough out onto a lightly floured work surface and knead for 10 minutes or until smooth and slightly springy. If using the food mixer, then knead on a medium speed for 6–8 minutes or until the dough is smooth and springy.
Continued …

RACHEL'S TIPS Place both the cumin and the coriander seeds in a non-stick pan over a medium–high heat and cook for a minute or so, tossing once or twice, until slightly darker in colour and toasted. Tip the toasted seeds into a mortar and crush with a pestle until fine, or place in a plastic bag and crush with a rolling pin instead.

To cook the dried beans, first soak them in plenty of cold water overnight. Drain and place in a saucepan filled with fresh water. Place on a high heat and bring to the boil, then reduce the heat and simmer for ¾–1 hour or until tender. Remove from the heat, drain in a colander and allow to cool.

Grease the bowl with olive oil and place the dough back into it, then cover with cling film and leave somewhere warm to rise for 1–2 hours or until doubled in size. (The time the dough takes to rise will depend on the yeast, the temperature of the water and the temperature of the room.)

Meanwhile, make the spiced cannellini bean dip. Place the beans in a food processor and whiz up with the ground spices, the garlic, parsley and olive oil until almost smooth. Stir in enough water (about 100ml/3½fl oz) to thin it out slightly – I like it to be the consistency of mayonnaise. Season to taste with salt and pepper, transfer to a serving bowl and set aside.

When the dough has finished rising, remove the cling film and knock back the dough by punching it to remove any air. Tip it out of the bowl onto your work surface.

Divide the dough into eight portions, then take one piece, dusting it and the worktop with flour, and roll it into a disc about 22cm (8½in) in diameter. Repeat with the remaining pieces of dough, keeping the unrolled pieces covered with a clean tea towel so that they don't dry out. I normally start cooking the flatbreads as soon as I have made the first one, so that while I'm rolling one, another is cooking in the pan (see next step).

Set a frying pan on a medium–high heat (no need to add any oil or butter) and allow it to get very hot, then place a flatbread in the pan and cook on each side for 1–2 minutes or until a few brown spots appear. Repeat with the remaining flatbreads. As each one is cooked, place on a board or plate, stacking them on top of each other, and cover with a clean tea towel or napkin to trap the steam and keep them soft and pliable.

Once cooked, serve warm or at room temperature with the spiced cannellini bean dip, garnished with parsley, freshly ground pepper and olive oil.

⊛ If you need more time, you can mix cold instead of warm water with the yeast and leave the dough in the fridge to rise. It will take 16–24 hours to double in size, giving you more flexibility about when to cook the flatbreads.

Once made, the flatbreads are best eaten on the day, but they can be kept, covered, somewhere dry and reheated in a moderate oven (preheated to 180°C/350°F/Gas mark 4) for a few minutes.

The cannellini bean dip can be stored in the fridge for a few days.

⊕ The quantities in this recipe could be easily halved or doubled, depending on how many people you're feeding.

⊡ Any leftover cannellini bean dip would be lovely spread on toast with a sprinkling of paprika and a drizzle of olive oil.

PINWHEELS

A smart way of using white yeast dough, pinwheels would make a luxurious snack.
They could be served with other items as an antipasto for an authentic Italian supper
and they'd also go well with the Chicken, Fennel and Orange Salad (see page 98).

Makes 20 pinwheels

215ml (7fl oz) warm water

1 tsp caster sugar

1½ tsp dried yeast or 15g (½oz) fresh yeast
or 1 x 7g sachet of fast-action yeast

350g (12oz) strong white flour, plus extra
for dusting

½ tsp salt

2 tbsp olive oil, plus extra for greasing

75g (3oz) mozzarella, grated

75g (3oz) Parmesan cheese, grated

75g (3oz) tapenade or pesto (see recipes opposite)

In a measuring jug, mix the warm water with the
sugar and yeast and leave to stand in a warm place
for 5 minutes or until the mixture is creamy.
If using fast-action yeast, there is no need to let
the mixture stand.

Sift the flour and salt into a large bowl, or the
bowl of an electric food mixer fitted with a dough
hook, and make a well in the centre. Add the
olive oil to the yeast mixture, then pour into the
well and mix together by hand or using the food
mixer until the dough has come together and is
slightly wet and sticky (add a little more water if
it seems too dry).

Knead for about 10 minutes or until the dough
is smooth and springy to the touch. (If kneading
in the electric food mixer, 5 minutes is usually
long enough.) Grease the bowl with olive oil and
put the dough back into it, then cover the top
tightly with cling film and place somewhere warm
to rise until doubled in size. This may take up to
2 or even (on a cold day) 3 hours.

Meanwhile, grease a large baking sheet with
olive oil and mix together the two grated cheeses
in a bowl.

When the dough has doubled in size, transfer
to a work surface dusted in flour. Sprinkle some
flour over the dough and roll it out into a rectangle
measuring roughly 20 x 25cm (8 x 10in). Spread
the tapenade or pesto over the dough to cover it,
then roll up like a Swiss roll, starting at one of the
longer edges.

Cut the rolled-up dough into 20 even-sized
slices, then place, cut side up, on the prepared
baking sheet, well spaced apart, and sprinkle each
one with the cheese. Set aside and leave to prove
for 20–30 minutes or until doubled in size.

Meanwhile, preheat the oven to 200°C (400°F),
Gas mark 6.

When the pinwheels have doubled in size,
place in the oven and bake for 10–15 minutes
or until cooked through and golden brown.

⊛ To give you more time, you can mix cold
instead of warm water with the yeast and leave the
dough in the fridge to double in size. It will take
16–24 hours for the first rising (when the dough
is in the bowl) and about 6 hours for the second
rising/proving (when the dough is shaped).

Once made, the pinwheels will keep in
an airtight container for up to four days. They are
best if reheated in a moderate oven (preheated to
180°C/350°F/Gas mark 4) for about 5 minutes.

⊕ The quantities in this recipe can easily be
multiplied.

PESTO

The distinctive peppery-floral taste of basil is what you associate with this traditional Italian sauce, yet you could replace it with another herb, such as parsley, rocket or wild garlic leaves. Pesto is wonderfully versatile: serve it with pasta, drizzle it over roasted or chargrilled vegetables, grilled meats or bruschetta, or spread it on toasted bread and top with roasted peppers and cheese.

Makes about 150g (5oz)

50g (2oz) basil, chopped
25g (1oz) Parmesan cheese, grated
25g (1oz) pine nuts
1–2 cloves of garlic, peeled and crushed
   or finely grated
75ml (3fl oz) olive oil, plus extra to cover
Salt

Place the basil, Parmesan cheese, pine nuts and garlic in a food processor and whiz together. With the machine still running, add the olive oil and blend to a smooth paste.

Add salt to taste, then pour into a sterilised jar (see tip below), and top up with enough olive oil to cover the pesto by 1cm (½in) before sealing the jar shut (see ✳ below). Store in the fridge.

TAPENADE

Tapenade is a classic Provençal sauce that combines olives, anchovies and capers. It is so useful to have in your fridge as it keeps for ages and can be used as a dip, on toast or over roasted vegetables or grilled meat. You can even thin it out with olive oil to make a salad dressing. For a vegetarian version, simply leave out the anchovies.

Makes about 150g (5oz)

100g (3½oz) pitted black olives
50g (2oz) tinned anchovy fillets
1 tbsp capers, rinsed
2 tsp Dijon mustard
1 tsp freshly squeezed lemon juice
Freshly ground black pepper
50ml (2fl oz) olive oil, plus extra to cover

Place the olives, anchovies, capers, mustard and lemon juice in a food processor and season with pepper. Whiz the ingredients together, then, with the machine still running, add the olive oil to form a thick paste. Place in a clean sterilised jar (see tip below) and top up with enough olive oil to cover the tapenade by 1cm (½in) before sealing the jar shut (see ✳ below).

✳ Stored in the fridge in an airtight jar, tapenade (and pesto) will keep for months. To prevent it going off, it must be covered with olive oil, so when you need some, just pour off the oil, spoon out the tapenade, then bang the jar on a surface to get rid of air bubbles and top up with olive oil again to cover.

RACHEL'S TIP To sterilise jars, either boil them in a saucepan of water for 5 minutes, put them through a dishwasher cycle or heat them in the oven (preheated to 150°C/300°F/Gas mark 2) for 10 minutes.

SUN-BLUSHED TOMATO PIZZA

Pizza is absolutely worth making yourself. Cooked in a very hot oven, it will be crisp on the outside and soft in the middle. Using sun-blushed tomatoes in the sauce gives you a wonderfully sweet and intense flavour which works perfectly with the doughy base. If you can't find them, roast or 'sun-dry' your own (see tips below) to use in the sauce.

Makes 4 pizzas

For the dough

215ml (7fl oz) warm water

1 tsp caster sugar

1½ tsp dried yeast or 15g (½oz) fresh yeast
    or 1 x 7g sachet fast-action yeast

350g (12oz) strong white flour, plus extra
    for dusting

½ tsp salt

2 tbsp olive oil, plus extra for greasing

75g (3oz) semolina or fine/medium polenta,
    for dusting

For the sun-blushed tomato sauce

50ml (2fl oz) olive oil

4 onions, peeled and finely chopped

8 cloves of garlic, peeled and crushed or
    finely grated

400g (14oz) sun-blushed (semi-sun-dried) tomatoes

1 tbsp sugar

4 tbsp tomato purée

Salt and freshly ground black pepper

For the topping

300g (11oz) Cheddar or Gruyère cheese, grated

300g (11oz) mozzarella, grated

First make the dough. In a measuring jug, mix the warm water with the sugar and yeast and leave to stand in a warm place for 5 minutes or until the mixture is creamy. If using fast-action yeast, there is no need to let the mixture stand.

Sift the flour and salt into a large bowl, or the bowl of an electric food mixer fitted with a dough hook, and make a well in the centre. Add the olive oil to the yeast mixture, then pour into the well and mix together by hand or using the food mixer until the dough has come together and is slightly wet and sticky (add a little more water if it seems too dry). Knead with your hands on a floured worktop for about 10 minutes (about 5 minutes in the food mixer) or until smooth and slightly springy to the touch.

Grease the bowl with olive oil and place the dough back in it, then cover with cling film and leave to rise for 1–2 hours or until doubled in size. If you gently press the dough with a floured fingertip and it does not spring back – that is, the dent made by your finger stays in the dough – then it is ready.

While the dough is rising, make the tomato sauce. Place a saucepan on a medium heat and *Continued …*

RACHEL'S TIPS To roast tomatoes for this sauce, you'll need 500g (1lb 2oz) of ripe tomatoes. Cut them in half and lay them, cut side up, in a roasting tin or baking tray. Drizzle olive oil over the top and sprinkle a little salt, pepper and sugar, then cook in the oven (preheated to 160°C/325°F/Gas mark 3) for ¾–1 hour or until soft and slightly wizened.

To 'sun-dry' tomatoes for the sauce, prepare 500g (1lb 2oz) of ripe tomatoes as in the first tip, then cook in the oven (preheated to 110°C/225°F/Gas mark ¼) for 5–6 hours.

add the oil. When the oil is hot, tip in the onion and garlic, season with salt and pepper and fry for 10 minutes, stirring regularly, or until the onion is softened and a little golden. Add the tomatoes, sugar, tomato purée and 100ml (3½fl oz) of water, then season with salt and pepper and cook, uncovered, for 10–15 minutes or until the tomatoes are tender.

Remove the sauce from the heat and transfer to a food processor, pulsing a few times until you have an almost smooth purée, then set aside while you make the pizza bases.

Preheat the oven to 240°C (475°F), Gas mark 9, or its highest setting, and place a pizza stone or baking sheet inside to get really hot.

Tip the dough onto a floured work surface and divide into four portions, then roll out each piece into a disc about 25cm (10in) in diameter and 3mm (⅛in) thick. (Keep the dough that you're not working with covered with an upturned bowl or a clean tea towel.)

Divide the tomato sauce between the pizza bases, spreading it out over the dough in an even layer, then sprinkle over the grated cheeses.

Place a pizza on a pizza paddle or upturned baking sheet sprinkled generously with semolina or polenta to stop the pizza base sticking and slide it, carefully but quickly, onto the hot stone or baking sheet in the oven. Bake for 4–12 minutes (the cooking time can vary hugely, depending on the oven you're using) or until golden brown and melted on top and crisp around the edges. Repeat with the remaining pizzas, cooking them one at a time.

✱ If you need more time, you can mix cold instead of warm water with the yeast and leave the dough in the fridge to rise. It will take 16–24 hours to double in size, giving you more flexibility about when to cook the pizzas.

Although nothing beats a freshly cooked pizza, these can be made in advance and frozen: take them out of the oven a couple of minutes before they're cooked and allow to cool before putting them in the freezer. Reheat from frozen in the oven (preheated to 220°C/425°F/Gas mark 7) for 5–10 minutes or until hot and crisp.

The tomato sauce can be made ahead too; it will keep well in the fridge for three days and in the freezer for up to three months.

⊖ You can make double quantities of the tomato sauce and store half for using as a topping for another type of pizza, such as the Parma Ham, Goat's Cheese and Red Onion Pizza (see page 37).

⊟ Use any leftover dough for making the Cheesy Chorizo Dough Balls (see page 40).

Any leftover tomato sauce can be saved for serving with pasta.

POTATO, MOZZARELLA AND ROSEMARY PIZZA

Potato is a fabulous ingredient to put on a pizza, and I'm not just saying that because I'm Irish! The soft cooked potatoes provide a delicious contrasting texture to the crisp pizza base.

Makes 4 pizzas

4 x 25cm (10in) diameter uncooked pizza bases
   (see page 32)
75g (3oz) semolina or medium/fine polenta,
   for dusting

For the topping

800g (1¾lb) potatoes, peeled, and halved
   if large, or cooked potatoes (see tip below)
50ml (2fl oz) olive oil
4 onions, peeled and sliced
6 cloves of garlic, peeled and crushed
   or finely grated
4 tbsp chopped rosemary leaves
400g (14oz) mozzarella, grated
Salt and freshly ground black pepper
24 black olives, pitted

First boil the potatoes (if cooking from scratch) for the topping. Place the potatoes in a large saucepan, cover with water and add 1 teaspoon of salt. Bring to the boil and cook for 20–25 minutes or until tender, then remove from the heat. Drain and allow to cool a little before cutting into thin slices.

Meanwhile, place a large frying pan on a medium heat and add the oil. When the oil is hot, add the onions, garlic and rosemary, and fry, stirring occasionally, for about 20 minutes or until the onions are golden brown. Remove from the heat and set aside.

Preheat the oven to 240°C (475°F), Gas mark 9, or its highest setting, and place a pizza or baking sheet inside to get really hot.

Sprinkle some of the mozzarella over each pizza base, then top with the potato slices and season with salt and pepper. Cover in the remaining mozzarella, dividing it up between each pizza, then top with the cooked onions followed by the olives.

Place a pizza on a pizza paddle or upturned baking sheet sprinkled generously with semolina or polenta to stop the pizza base sticking and slide it, carefully but quickly, onto the hot stone or baking sheet in the oven. Bake for 4–12 minutes (the cooking time can vary hugely, depending on the oven you're using) or until golden brown and melted on top and crisp around the edges. Repeat with the remaining pizzas, cooking them one at a time.

⊖⁺ The quantities in the pizza topping can be halved to cover two pizza bases.

RACHEL'S TIP Making this pizza is a great way of using leftover cooked potatoes, whether boiled or roasted. If you have any lurking in the fridge, use these instead of cooking potatoes from scratch. If using floury potatoes, such as Golden Wonders, peel them after boiling, as they tend to absorb too much water if cooked without their skins, and collapse once cooked.

LAMB, FETA AND CHARD PIZZA

Chard is such a lovely green vegetable, with a distinctive mineral taste that works so well this pizza, to which the spring onions bring sweetness and the feta its characteristic salty tang. The lamb combines particularly well with these flavours, but if you've any leftover cooked chicken (see pages 82, 90 and 98), that would make a good substitute.

Makes 4 pizzas

4 x 25cm (10in) diameter uncooked pizza bases
   (see page 32)
75g (3oz) semolina or medium/fine polenta,
   for dusting

For the topping

400g (14oz) chard
6 tbsp olive oil
12 spring onions, trimmed and finely sliced
4 cloves garlic, peeled and crushed
   or finely grated
Salt and freshly ground black pepper
2 tbsp cumin seeds, toasted and ground
   (see tip below)
4 tbsp chopped mint
400g (14oz) feta cheese
400g (14oz) cooked lamb (see page 146),
   cut or shredded into thin bite-sized pieces
   5–6cm (2–2½in) long

To make the topping, first chop the stalks off the chard leaves and cut these into 2cm (¾in) lengths, then shred the leaves.

Next place a frying pan on a high heat and pour in 2 tablespoons of the olive oil. When the oil is hot, tip in the chard stalks, spring onions and garlic, season with salt and pepper and cook for 3 minutes. Add the ground cumin, shredded chard leaves and chopped mint and cook for a further 2 minutes or until the chard is tender. Taste for seasoning, adding more salt and pepper if necessary.

Preheat the oven to 240°C (475°F), Gas mark 9, or its highest setting, and place a pizza stone or baking sheet inside to get really hot.

Spread the chard mixture all over each pizza base, then crumble over the feta and top with the cooked lamb. Season with salt and pepper and drizzle over the remaining olive oil.

Place a pizza on a pizza paddle or upturned baking sheet sprinkled generously with semolina or polenta to stop the pizza base sticking and slide it, carefully but quickly, onto the hot stone or baking sheet in the oven. Bake for 4–12 minutes (the cooking time can vary hugely, depending on the oven you're using) or until golden on top and light golden underneath. Repeat with the remaining pizzas, cooking them one at a time.

The quantities in the pizza topping can be halved to cover two pizza bases.

RACHEL'S TIP To toast the cumin seeds, place in a small, non-stick saucepan over a medium–high heat and cook for a minute or so, tossing once or twice, until slightly darker in colour and toasted. Tip the toasted seeds into a mortar and crush with a pestle until fine, or place in a plastic bag and crush with a rolling pin instead.

PARMA HAM, GOAT'S CHEESE AND RED ONION PIZZA

Just a few slices of ham per pizza is enough of this fabulous ingredient – with such an intense flavour, a little goes a long way. The red onions are roasted to enhance their sweetness, the perfect complement to the savoury goat's cheese.

Makes 4 pizzas

4 x 25cm (10in) diameter uncooked pizza bases (see page 32)

75g (3oz) semolina or medium/fine polenta, for dusting

For the topping

2 red onions, peeled and each cut into 8 or 10 wedges

4 sprigs of thyme

6 tbsp olive oil

Salt and freshly ground black pepper

1 quantity of sun-blushed tomato sauce (see page 32)

400g (14oz) goat's cheese, cut or broken into 1–2cm (½–¾in) chunks

12 slices of Parma or Serrano ham, torn into slightly smaller pieces

Preheat the oven to 240°C (475°F), Gas mark 9, or its highest setting, and place a pizza stone or baking sheet inside to get really hot.

Place the onion wedges in a roasting tin with the thyme. Drizzle with 2 tablespoons of the oil, season with salt and pepper and roast for 10–15 minutes until the onion is tender and browned around the edges. Remove from the oven and set aside.

Spread the tomato sauce over the pizza bases, then add 4–5 roasted onion wedges to each pizza. Dot with the goat's cheese and pieces of ham, then drizzle with the remaining olive oil and season with a little pepper.

Place a pizza on a pizza paddle or upturned baking sheet sprinkled generously with semolina or polenta to stop the pizza base sticking and slide it, carefully but quickly, onto the hot stone or baking sheet in the oven. Bake for 4–12 minutes (the cooking time can vary hugely, depending on the oven you're using) or until golden brown on top and crisp around the edges. Repeat with the remaining pizzas, cooking them one at a time.

The quantities in the pizza topping can be halved to cover two pizza bases.

CHEESY CHORIZO DOUGH BALLS

A serious favourite with our children, these are even more wicked and delicious if dipped in garlic butter. These are best eaten warm, so reheat them if they've cooled – the perfect snack to enjoy with a movie, for instance. This recipe is also a great way of using leftover bread or pizza dough (see page 32). Make the recipe as below, keeping the ratio of chorizo to Gruyère roughly the same (two-thirds chorizo to Gruyère) if you're using different quantities for the filling.

Makes 40 balls

For the dough

215ml (7fl oz) warm water

1 tsp caster sugar

1½ tsp dried yeast or 15g (½oz) fresh yeast or 1 x 7g sachet fast-action yeast

350g (12oz) strong white flour, plus extra for dusting

½ tsp salt

2 tbsp olive oil, plus extra for greasing

75g (3oz) semolina or fine/medium polenta, for dusting

For the filling

100g (3½oz) chorizo, cut into roughly 5mm (¼in) cubes

150g (5oz) Gruyère cheese, cut into roughly 5mm (¼in) cubes

3 tsp chopped thyme leaves

For the garlic butter (optional)

100g (3½oz) butter, softened

2–4 cloves of garlic, peeled and crushed or finely grated

1 generous tbsp chopped mixed herbs, such as parsley, chives and tarragon

In a measuring jug, mix the warm water with the sugar and yeast and leave to stand in a warm place for 5 minutes or until the mixture becomes creamy. If using fast-action yeast, there is no need to let the mixture stand.

Sift the flour and salt into a large bowl, or the bowl of an electric food mixer fitted with a dough hook, and make a well in the centre. Add the olive oil to the yeast mixture, then pour into the well and mix together by hand or using the food mixer until the dough has come together and is slightly wet and sticky (add a little more water if it seems too dry). Knead by hand on a floured worktop for 10 minutes (8 minutes on a medium speed in the food mixer) or until the dough is smooth and slightly springy to the touch.

Grease the bowl with olive oil and place the dough back in it, then cover with cling film and leave to sit in a warm part of your kitchen for 1–2 hours or until more than doubled in size. (Depending on how warm your kitchen is, it may take longer.)

Once the dough has risen, transfer it to a work surface dusted in flour. Divide the dough into 40 balls, then roll each out into a disc measuring about 5cm (2½in) in diameter. Divide the chorizo, Gruyère and thyme between the discs, then enclose the filling within the discs, sealing tightly shut, and gently shape into balls.

Place the filled dough balls, well spaced apart, on 2–3 greased baking trays, then cover with clean tea towels and leave to prove for 20–30 minutes or until doubled in size.

Meanwhile, preheat the oven to 200°C (400°F), Gas mark 6, and make the garlic butter (if using).

Cream the butter in a bowl, then mix in the garlic and herbs.

When the dough balls have doubled in size, place in the oven and bake for 8–10 minutes or until cooked through and light golden all over. (Unless you have a fan oven, you will need to cook the dough balls in 2–3 batches.) Don't worry if some of the cheese oozes out!

If using the garlic butter, melt it first in a saucepan, then either pour over the dough balls to serve or dip them into the melted butter.

✳ To give you more time, you can mix cold instead of warm water with the yeast and leave the dough in the fridge to double in size. It will take 16–24 hours for the first rising (when the dough is in the bowl) and about 6 hours for the second rising/proving (when the dough is shaped).

Though best eaten fresh, these will keep for up to two days. Reheat for a few minutes in a moderate oven (preheated to 180°C/350°F/Gas mark 4). They can otherwise be stored in the freezer and reheated from frozen for 10 minutes.

⊖ The quantities in this recipe can be easily to halved or multiplied for serving fewer or more people.

WHITE YEAST BREAD

A simple white bread is the mainstay of any baker's repertoire. The basic recipe, however, can be endlessly modified, by adding ingredients to the dough (spices, herbs, cheese, olives, caramelised onion, nuts, candied fruit, chocolate), by shaping it (long, round or plaited) or sprinkling the top with seeds, herbs or salt before baking. However you ring the changes, nothing beats a homemade loaf, warm, fragrant and fresh from the oven.

Makes 2 x 450g (1lb) loaves
425ml (15fl oz) warm water
2 tsp caster sugar
3 tsp dried yeast or 30g (1¼oz) fresh yeast
   or 2 x 7g sachets of fast-action yeast
700g (1lb 9oz) strong white flour, plus extra
   for dusting (optional)
1 tsp salt
50ml (2fl oz) olive oil, plus extra for greasing
1 egg, beaten, and poppy or sesame seeds (optional)

In a measuring jug, mix the warm water with the sugar and yeast and leave to stand in a warm place for 5 minutes or until the mixture is creamy. If using fast-action yeast, skip the standing time.

Sift the flour and salt into a large bowl, or the bowl of an electric food mixer fitted with a dough hook, and make a well in the centre. Add the olive oil to the yeast mixture, then pour into the well and mix together by hand or using the food mixer until the dough has come together and is slightly wet and sticky (add a little more water if it seems too dry).

Knead by hand for about 10 minutes (5 minutes in the food mixer) or until the dough is smooth and springy to the touch. Grease the bowl with olive oil and put the dough back into it, then cover the top tightly with cling film and place somewhere warm to rise for up to 2 hours (up to 3 hours on a cold day) or until doubled in size.

When the dough has more than doubled in size, knock back and knead again for 2–3 minutes. Leave to relax for 10 minutes.

Divide the dough in half and shape into two loaves, then transfer to a baking sheet and cover with a clean tea towel. Allow to prove in a warm

place for 20–30 minutes or until the dough has doubled in size. When fully risen, it should leave a dent when you gently press it with your finger.

While the bread is proving, preheat the oven to 220°C (425°F), Gas mark 7.

Dust the top of each loaf with flour or gently brush with beaten egg and sprinkle with poppy or sesame seeds (if using), then bake in the oven for 40–45 minutes. Turn the heat down to 200°C (400°F), Gas mark 6, after 15 minutes for the remaining cooking time. When cooked, the bread should sound hollow when tapped on the base. Transfer to a wire rack to cool.

⊘ **White yeast rolls:** Divide the dough into smaller portions to make rolls. Prove as above, then dust with flour or brush with egg wash, sprinkle with poppy/sesame seeds and bake for 10–15 minutes, then 15 minutes at the reduced temperature.

✳ Letting the bread rise slowly not only improves its texture and flavour but means you can start preparing it in advance. Mix cold instead of warm water with the yeast and leave the kneaded dough to rise in the fridge – it will take 16–24 hours to double in size. When the dough has been shaped into loaves, leave to prove for 8 hours in the fridge.

The bread will keep, wrapped, for a couple of days. Alternatively, slice the loaf, place in an airtight bag and freeze it: it will keep for up to one month.

▢ Use the end of a loaf to make breadcrumbs. Stale bread also works well in the Cheesy Bread Gratin (see page 119) or the White Chocolate and Raspberry Bread and Butter Pudding (see page 230).

THREE CHEESE BREAD

The three cheeses included here each bring their distinctive flavour to this bread. An ideal accompaniment to soups and stews, it is moist and flavourful enough to be eaten on its own or with a little butter. This recipe is a good way of using up ends of cheese; you can substitute with any other hard varieties that you may have in your fridge, in any combination you like.

Makes 1 loaf

215ml (7fl oz) warm water

1 tsp caster sugar

1½ tsp dried yeast or 15g (½oz) fresh yeast or 1 x 7g sachet fast-action yeast

350g (12oz) strong white flour, plus extra for dusting

½ tsp salt

2 tbsp olive oil, plus extra for greasing

75g (3oz) Parmesan cheese, grated

75g (3oz) Gruyère cheese, grated

75g (3oz) Cheddar cheese, grated

Equipment

23cm (9in) diameter baking tin

In a measuring jug, mix the warm water with the sugar and yeast and leave to stand in a warm place for 5 minutes until the mixture is creamy. If using fast-action yeast, there is no need to let the mixture stand.

Sift the flour and salt into a large bowl, or the bowl of an electric food mixer fitted with a dough hook and make a well in the centre. Add the olive oil to the yeast mixture, then pour the yeast mixture into the well and mix together by hand or using the food mixer until the dough has come together and is slightly wet and sticky (add a little more water if it seems too dry).

Knead by hand for about 10 minutes (5 minutes in the food mixer) or until the dough is smooth and springy to the touch. Grease the bowl with oil and put the dough back into it, then cover the top tightly with cling film and place somewhere warm to rise for up to 2 hours (up to 3 hours on a cold day) or until doubled in size.

Meanwhile, grease the baking tin and mix the grated cheeses together in a bowl.

When the dough has finished rising, transfer it to your worktop. Dust the dough and the worktop with flour to prevent the dough from sticking, then roll it out into a rectangle measuring 20 x 30cm (8 x 12in) and 3–4mm (⅛in) thick.

Sprinkle the grated cheeses over the rolled-out dough to cover it. Then, using both hands and starting at one of the long ends, roll up the dough (not too tightly) so that it resembles a Swiss roll. Using a sharp knife (serrated if possible) that you have dusted with flour, cut the loaf/roll into eight slices, each about 3.5cm (1½in) thick.

Arrange seven of these slices, cut side up, around the side of the tin and one in the middle, again cut side up. The gaps between the cheesy swirls will close as the bread proves. Cover with a clean tea towel and leave to prove for about 30 minutes or until doubled in size.

Meanwhile, preheat the oven to 220°C (425°F), Gas mark 7 (see tip below). Place the loaf in the oven and bake for 20–25 minutes or until golden

RACHEL'S TIP Turn the oven temperature down to 200°C (400°F), Gas mark 6, at any stage during cooking if you think the top of the bread is golden enough and don't want it to burn. Some ovens cook more rapidly than others.

brown and crusty on top. At this stage you can take the tin out of the oven, carefully tip the loaf out of the tin, then place the bread back in the oven for a further 10–15 minutes or until cooked. When cooked the bread should sound hollow when tapped on the base. Remove from the oven and place on a wire rack to cool.

✳ To start preparing the bread in advance, you can mix cold instead of warm water with the yeast and leave the dough in the fridge to double in size. It will take 16–24 hours for the first rising (when the dough is in the bowl) and about 6 hours for the second rising/proving (when the dough has been cut up and placed in the tin).

This bread will keep in an airtight container for up to three days or in the freezer, well wrapped up, for up to a month. Once defrosted, it can be reheated for a few minutes in a moderate oven (preheated to 180°C/350°F/Gas mark 4).

⊖ You could double the quantities in this recipe, dividing the dough in two after it has risen – to make two rectangles that you then roll and cut up as above – and filling two baking tins.

CARAMELISED ONION AND ROSEMARY BREAD

The slow-cooked, caramelised onions, fragrant from the rosemary, are what gives this bread its fantastic flavour. It's best enjoyed warm with olive oil to dunk it into.

Makes 1 loaf
For the dough
215ml (7fl oz) warm water
1 tsp caster sugar
1½ tsp dried yeast or 15g (½oz) fresh yeast
    or 1 x 7g sachet fast-action yeast
350g (12oz) strong white flour, plus extra
    for dusting
½ tsp salt
2 tbsp olive oil, plus extra for greasing

For the onion mixture
2 tbsp olive oil, plus extra for brushing
500g (1lb 2oz) onions, peeled and sliced
1 tbsp chopped rosemary leaves
Salt and freshly ground black pepper

Equipment
900g (2lb) loaf tin

In a measuring jug, mix the warm water with the sugar and yeast and leave to stand in a warm place for 5 minutes or until the mixture is creamy. If using fast-action yeast, there is no need to let the mixture stand.

Sift the flour and salt into a large bowl, or the bowl of an electric food mixer fitted with a dough hook, and make a well in the centre. Add the olive oil to the yeast mixture, then pour it into the well and mix together by hand or using the food mixer until the dough comes together and is slightly wet and sticky (add a little more water if it seems too dry).

Knead by hand for about 10 minutes (about 5 minutes in the food mixer) or until the dough is smooth and springy to the touch. Grease the bowl with olive oil and put the dough back into it, then cover the top tightly with cling film and place somewhere warm to rise for up to 2 hours (even 3 hours on a cold day) or until doubled in size.

While the dough is rising, cook the onions. Place a large saucepan or frying pan on a medium heat and add the olive oil. When the oil is hot, add the onions and rosemary and season. Stir to mix and when the mixture is beginning to sizzle, turn the heat down to low and cook, stirring occasionally, for ¾–1 hour or until deep golden. Remove from the heat, season to taste and allow to cool.

When the dough has doubled in size, tip the cooked onions over the top of the dough in the bowl and, making a fist with your hand, punch the dough to knock it back while at the same time mixing in the onions.

Transfer the dough, and any stray onions, from the bowl to a worktop lightly dusted in flour. (If there are clumps of escaping onions, you may need to tuck them back into the dough with your fingertips.) Form the dough into an oval shape almost the length of the tin. Brush the sides of the tin liberally with olive oil and transfer the dough to the tin. Brush the top of the loaf with more olive oil and leave to prove in a warm place for about 30 minutes or until the dough has doubled in size.

Meanwhile, preheat the oven to 220°C (425°F), Gas mark 7.

Place the loaf in the oven and bake for 10 minutes, then turn the oven temperature down to 200°C (400°F), Gas mark 6, and continue to bake for 35–40 minutes or until golden brown on top. When the loaf is cooked, it should come out of the tin easily and sound hollow when tapped on the base. Remove from the oven and allow to cool for a few minutes, then remove from the tin, if you haven't already, and place on a wire rack to cool completely.

✳ To start preparing the bread in advance, you can mix cold instead of warm water with the yeast and leave the dough in the fridge to double in size. It will take 16–24 hours for the first rising (when the dough is in the bowl) and about 6 hours for the second rising/proving (when the dough is shaped).

Though best eaten fresh, this bread will keep for up to three days in an airtight container and of course can be toasted or popped into a moderate oven (preheated to 180°C/350°F/Gas mark 4) for a few minutes to reheat.

⊝ You can double up the quantities in this recipe (including the onion mixture) to make two loaves. Simply divide the dough into two portions after you have added the onions, then shape into loaves and place in separate tins.

FISH & SHELLFISH

SMOKED SALMON AND LEMON RISOTTO WITH ASPARAGUS

✳ ⊖ ⊡

I find risottos so soothing to cook. Once started, they need only a gentle stir and the regular addition of hot stock. The dill and lemon in this recipe offset the rich salmon and creamy rice, while the asparagus offers welcome texture contrast with its own distinctive flavour.

Serves 4–6

2 tbsp olive oil
1 onion, peeled and finely chopped
1 clove of garlic, peeled and finely chopped
350g (12oz) risotto rice
1 litre (1¾ pints) chicken stock (see page 20) or fish stock
200ml (7fl oz) white wine
Juice of ½–1 lemon
50g (2oz) crème fraîche
25g (1oz) butter
2 tbsp chopped dill
170g (6oz) smoked salmon, thinly sliced
75g (3oz) Parmesan cheese, finely grated
Salt and freshly ground black pepper
6 stalks of asparagus, woody ends snapped off and discarded, spears sliced at an angle into roughly 3cm (1¼in) lengths
1 tsp finely grated lemon zest, to serve

Place the olive oil in large saucepan on a low heat. When the oil is hot, add the onion and garlic, then cover the pan with a lid and cook for 8–10 minutes or until soft but not browned. Turn the heat up to medium, add the rice and stir for about 2 minutes or until the rice is well coated. Heat through the stock in another saucepan and keep at a very gentle simmer.

Pour the wine into the rice mixture. Bring to the boil, then lower the heat and allow to simmer and reduce for about 3 minutes. Add a ladleful of stock and half the lemon juice to the rice and continue to stir until most of the stock has been absorbed, then add another ladleful and continue stirring. Continue in this way until all of the stock has been incorporated

and the rice is creamy and just al dente – it should take no more than 25 minutes.

Stir in the crème fraîche, butter, dill, smoked salmon and 50g (2oz) of the Parmesan cheese, then season with salt and pepper and add more lemon juice if necessary. Remove from the heat: the risotto should be wet and loose in consistency, not thick and porridge-like.

While you are cooking the risotto, cook the asparagus in boiling salted water for 2–3 minutes or just until tender, then drain and set aside.

Serve the risotto on warmed plates or in shallow bowls with the asparagus scattered over the top. Add a sprinkling of lemon zest and plenty of black pepper, and scatter over the remaining grated Parmesan.

✳ Once the risotto is cooked it's best served immediately, but if you want to prepare it a couple of hours in advance, you can cook the risotto until roughly two-thirds done (taking about 15 minutes and using about two-thirds of the stock), when it will still have a definite bite. Tip it out of the saucepan onto a baking tray and spread it out to cool (to stop it cooking any more). When you are ready to serve the risotto, you can tip it back into the saucepan and finish cooking it as above.

It's important to refrigerate any leftover rice soon after cooking; it can then be stored in the fridge for a maximum of three days.

⊖ You can double the quantities in this recipe to serve more people.

⊡ Any leftover risotto can be made into arancini (see page 53).

EASY ARANCINI WITH CRÈME FRAÎCHE HERB SAUCE

Arancini are one of my favourite Sicilian foods – balls of delicious risotto that are coated in breadcrumbs and fried so that they are crisp on the outside but melting and soft in the middle. I usually prepare extra risotto (see page 50) so that I have enough for making arancini. They are so good, in fact, that for me risotto is simply part one of the story and arancini part two when the plot gets even better!

Makes about 15 balls/Serves 3–4
350g (12oz) Smoked Salmon and Lemon Risotto
  (see page 50 – without the asparagus)
25g (1oz) Parmesan cheese, finely grated
50g (2oz) breadcrumbs
4–6 tbsp olive oil

For the crème fraîche sauce
250g (9oz) crème fraîche
1 tbsp lemon juice
1 tbsp chopped dill
1 tbsp chopped chives
Salt and freshly ground black pepper

Place the risotto in a large bowl and stir in the Parmesan until well mixed. Spread out the breadcrumbs on a plate.

Use your hands to roll the risotto mixture into about 30 balls each the size of a ping-pong ball,

then roll in the breadcrumbs to coat, and place on a tray. Put the risotto balls in the fridge to chill for at least 30 minutes or overnight, if you like.

In a bowl, combine the crème fraiche, lemon juice and herbs to make a dipping sauce, seasoning with salt and pepper to taste.

To cook the arancini, place a large frying pan on a high heat and add 2 tablespoons of olive oil. When the oil is hot, add a few of the arancini. Fry for about 4 minutes, turning occasionally, until golden brown all over.

When cooked, transfer to a serving plate lined with kitchen paper to allow the arancini to drain, then repeat with the remaining risotto balls, adding more oil as needed. Serve warm with the crème fraîche sauce.

(∗) The crème fraîche sauce can be made a few hours ahead and kept in the fridge until needed.

POTATO, SMOKED SALMON AND DILL TART

Dill's unique aniseed-like flavour works well with smoked salmon or potatoes, so I've combined all three for a gorgeous tart that's just as good served warm or cold.

Serves 6

For the pastry tart case
200g (7oz) plain flour
Pinch of salt
100g (3½oz) chilled butter, diced
½–1 egg, beaten

For the filling
200g (7oz) peeled potatoes, halved if large
Salt and freshly ground black pepper
25g (1oz) butter
1 onion, peeled and diced
2 eggs
200ml (7fl oz) double or regular cream
100g (3½oz) smoked salmon, cut into roughly
    1cm (½in) pieces
1 generous tbsp chopped dill

Equipment
23cm (9in) diameter, fluted, loose-bottomed
tart tin with 2cm (¾in) sides

To make the pastry
If making by hand, sift the flour and salt into a bowl and rub in the butter until the mixture resembles coarse breadcrumbs. Add half the beaten egg and bring the dough together with your hands, adding a little more egg if it is too dry. If you are using a food processor, sift in the flour and salt then add the butter. Whiz for a few seconds, then add half the beaten egg and whiz for a few more seconds (avoid over-processing the dough) until it comes together, adding more egg if necessary. Reserve the remaining beaten egg. Without kneading the dough, shape it into a round, 1–2cm (½–¾in) thick, using your hands to flatten it. Wrap in cling film and chill for about 30 minutes. Preheat the

oven to 180°C (350°F), Gas mark 4.

Take the pastry out of the fridge and place it between two sheets of cling film (each bigger than your tart tin). Roll out the pastry to about 3mm (⅛in) thick, keeping it in a round shape and large enough to line the base and sides of the tin.

Removing the top layer of cling film, place the pastry upside down (cling film side facing up) in the tart tin. (There's no need to flour or grease the tin.) Press the pastry into the edges of the tin, with the cling film still attached to the dough, and use your thumb to 'cut' the pastry along the edge of the tin for a neat finish. Patch up any holes or gaps in the pastry with spare pieces of dough. Remove the cling film and chill the pastry shell in the fridge for 15 minutes or in the freezer for 5 minutes.

Remove the pastry shell from the fridge or freezer and line with greaseproof paper or baking parchment, letting plenty of paper come up over the sides. Fill with baking beans or dried pulses, and bake 'blind' for 20–25 minutes or until the pastry feels just dry to the touch on the base.

Remove the paper and beans, brush with a little of the remaining beaten egg and return to the oven for 3 minutes. Again, if there are little holes or cracks in the pastry, patch them up with leftover dough before returning to the oven, so that the filling doesn't leak out. Take the tin out of the oven and set it aside while you make the filling.

To make the filling
Place the potatoes in a saucepan, cover with cold water and add a pinch of salt. Bring to the boil and cook the potatoes for 10–20 minutes or until tender when pierced with fork. Drain, then cut into slices about 5mm (¼in) thick. Preheat the oven to 180°C (350°F), Gas mark 4.

Melt the butter in a frying pan on a medium heat until foaming. Add the onion and sauté for about 10 minutes or until soft and lightly golden, then remove from the heat.

In a bowl, whisk together the eggs and cream and season. Spread the cooked onions in the tart case and top with a layer of sliced potatoes. Season, then sprinkle over the dill and arrange smoked salmon slices on top. Carefully pour the egg mixture over the fish and potatoes, through a sieve, and bake the tart for 30–40 minutes or until golden brown on top and just set in the centre.

Take out of the oven and allow to sit for 2–3 minutes before removing from the tin, then serve warm or cool with a watercress salad on the side.

(✳) The dough, wrapped in cling film, will keep in the fridge for up to 24 hours; it can also be frozen for up to three months. The uncooked tart case, well wrapped, will keep for several weeks in the freezer. It can also be blind baked a day in advance (kept covered until filled). Use it for the Cheese, Tomato and Basil Tart (see page 120) and Smoked Mackerel Tart (see page 58).

SUNSHINE FISH CURRY

Turmeric, with its brilliant shade of yellow, is what makes this golden curry look like sunshine on the plate. As with all dishes that use chilli, the level of heat is really up to you. If you'd like it hotter, you can use the whole chilli and not deseed it (the seeds being where most of the heat comes from), or you can leave it out altogether if you prefer.

Serves 6

6 skinned fillets of white fish, such as cod, haddock, whiting, pollock or ling

1 tsp cumin seeds, toasted and finely ground (see tip below)

1 tsp coriander seeds, toasted and finely ground (see tip below)

1 tsp turmeric

¾ tsp salt

2 tbsp sunflower oil

1 onion, peeled and chopped

1 x 400ml tin of coconut milk, whisked in a bowl to remove any lumps

½–1 fresh red chilli pepper, deseeded (optional) and thinly sliced (optional)

Squeeze of lemon juice

Place the fish on a plate or in a wide, shallow bowl. Mix the ground, toasted seeds with the turmeric and salt, then scatter over the fish, making sure the fillets are fully coated in the mixture.

Place a wide saucepan (or large frying pan) on a medium heat and pour in the sunflower oil. When the oil is hot, add the chopped onion and sauté for 7–10 minutes or until completely softened and a little golden around the edges.

Lay the fish pieces on top of the onion, making sure to scrape any leftover seeds and spices from the plate into the pan. Cook the fish on each side for 2–3 minutes or until light golden (you might need to turn the heat up so that the oil sizzles slightly).

Pour in the coconut milk and add the chilli (if using). Bring to the boil, then reduce the heat and simmer for 5–10 minutes or until the fish is cooked all the way through. To finish, add a squeeze of lemon juice and a little more salt if necessary. Serve immediately with the Sesame Pak Choi (see page 198).

RACHEL'S TIP To toast the seeds, place in a small, non-stick pan over a medium–high heat and cook for a minute or so, tossing once or twice, until slightly darker in colour and toasted. Tip the toasted seeds into a mortar and crush with a pestle until fine, or place in a plastic bag and crush with a rolling pin instead.

SMOKED MACKEREL TART

Mackerel is one of my favourite types of fish – rich and oily and incredibly good for you. It takes especially well to the smoking process, its flesh soaking up the smoky aromas. I use smoked mackerel in so many different dishes but I love the simplicity of this tart. The filling is creamy and silky smooth, with a touch of sweetness from the tomatoes and the whole tart infused by the pungent smokiness of the fish.

Serves 6

1 shortcrust pastry tart case, cooked 'blind' (see page 54)

For the filling

40g (1½oz) butter

1 large onion (about 300g/11oz), peeled and finely chopped

2 eggs

200ml (7fl oz) double or regular cream

Salt and freshly ground black pepper

1 tbsp chopped chives

4 ripe tomatoes, peeled (see tip below), deseeded (optional) and chopped

500g (1lb 2oz) smoked mackerel (about 5 fillets), skin removed and flesh broken into chunky flakes

Preheat the oven to 180°C (350°F), Gas mark 4.

To make the filling for the tart, melt the butter in a saucepan, then add the onion, cover with a lid and sweat over a gentle heat for 6–8 minutes or until completely softened but not browned. Remove from the heat and set aside to allow to cool.

In a large bowl, whisk together the eggs and cream and season with salt and pepper. Spread the cooked onions out in the tart case, then sprinkle over the chives and place the chopped tomatoes and mackerel pieces on top. Carefully pour the egg mixture over the tomatoes and fish through a sieve (to catch any unbeaten bits of egg).

Transfer to the oven and bake for about 35 minutes or until golden on top and just set in the middle. Allow the tart to sit for 2–3 minutes before removing from the tin, and serve either warm or at room temperature.

✱ The cooked tart can be made ahead and stored in the fridge, where it will keep for 24 hours. Reheat, if you like, in a moderate oven (preheated to 180°C/350°F/Gas mark 4) for about 10 minutes to warm through.

▢ Any leftover smoked mackerel tart would be perfect for a lunchbox or picnic.

RACHEL'S TIP To peel the tomatoes, use a sharp knife to score a cross in the base of each one, cutting through the skin. Place the tomatoes in a bowl and cover with boiling water, leaving them in the water for 15–20 seconds. Drain and rinse in cold water, then peel away the skin – it should come away very easily.

CHERMOULA FISH TAGINE

Chermoula is a staple of North African cooking. Packed with flavour, it is used as a marinade and sauce for grilled meat and fish. This tagine includes preserved lemons, which are delicious and so easy to make. Preparing them in the traditional way takes months, but my speedier preserved lemons are ready in less than an hour!

Serves 4–6

1kg (2lb 3oz) skinned fillets of white fish, such as cod, haddock, whiting, ling or pollock, cut into 2cm (¾in) pieces

3 tbsp olive oil

1 red onion, peeled and finely chopped

1 carrot, peeled and finely chopped

2 sticks of celery, trimmed and finely chopped

½ preserved lemon (see opposite), finely chopped

1 x 400g tin of chopped tomatoes, or 400g (14oz) tomatoes, peeled (see tip on p58) and chopped

600g (1lb 5oz) potatoes, peeled and cut into 2cm (¾in) pieces

Salt and freshly ground black pepper

2 tbsp roughly chopped coriander, to serve

For the chermoula marinade

3 cloves of garlic, peeled and chopped

1 fresh red chilli pepper, deseeded (optional) and chopped

1 tsp salt

Small handful of coriander (leaves and stems)

Pinch of saffron threads

2 tsp cumin seeds, toasted and finely ground (see tip below)

4 tbsp olive oil

Juice of 1 lemon

First make the marinade. Using a pestle and mortar, pound together the garlic, chilli, salt, coriander, saffron and cumin seeds. Add the olive oil and lemon juice and grind together to form a loose paste. Alternatively, use a hand-held blender and pulse the ingredients to form a paste.

Reserve 2 teaspoons of the chermoula and place the rest in a large bowl or sealable plastic bag. Add the fish pieces, turning them in the marinade to ensure they are well coated, and leave to marinate for at least an hour, preferably two.

Place a casserole dish or large saucepan on a medium heat and add the olive oil. When the oil is hot, add the onion, carrot and celery. Cook the vegetables for 8–10 minutes or until softened, then stir in the reserved chermoula and the preserved lemon, tomatoes and potatoes. Pour in 300ml (½ pint) of water, season and bring to the boil. Reduce the heat and simmer, covered, for 10–15 minutes or until the potatoes are almost cooked.

Add the fish with every bit of the chermoula marinade, and simmer very gently for a further 4–5 minutes or until the fish is opaque all the way through. Divide the tagine between bowls and scatter with chopped coriander. Serve immediately with chunks of fresh crusty bread.

⁎ Once the fish is cooked, it's best to serve the tagine straight away. If you want to prepare it ahead of time, however, cook it up to the point of adding the fish, let it cool and keep it, covered, in the fridge for up to three days. Reheat and then add the fish.

⊕ The quantities in this recipe can be halved or multiplied.

RACHEL'S TIP To toast the seeds, cook for a minute or so in a small, non-stick pan on a medium–high heat, tossing once or twice, until slightly darker in colour and fragrant. Tip them into a mortar and crush with a pestle until fine.

QUICK PRESERVED LEMONS

These salty lemon skins are a quintessential part of many North African recipes, used in tagines, salads and couscous dishes.

2 tbsp salt
2 lemons, quartered
Olive oil, to cover

Pour 250ml (9fl oz) of water into a small saucepan, add the salt and bring to the boil. Add the lemons, then reduce the heat and cook, covered, for 30–40 minutes or until the lemon rind is tender. Remove from the heat and allow to cool. Once cooled, scrape away and discard the lemon pulp. Place the lemon skins in a sterilised jar (see tip below), cover in olive oil and seal shut. The preserved lemons will keep for a couple of months in the fridge.

(✳) To sterilise jars, boil them in water for 5 minutes, put them through a dishwasher cycle or heat them in the oven (preheated to 150°C/300°F/Gas mark 2) for 10 minutes.

(–+) You can easily multiply the quantities: simply allow 1 tablespoon of salt per extra lemon.

SMOKED HADDOCK PIE

Made with well-loved ingredients – mashed potato, bacon and peas – there is nothing more comforting than a fish pie. Yet comfort food is no less impressive and certainly no less delicious just because it's familiar. This fish pie keeps it simple, the smoked haddock taking centre stage, with one of its favourite companions, boiled eggs, adding a nice contrast in texture. You can easily make this dish the day before as it will keep, unbaked, in the fridge, making cooking it the next day supremely easy.

Serves 6–8

4 eggs
1 litre (1¾ pints) milk
600g (1lb 5oz) smoked haddock fillets
   (preferably undyed)
25g (1oz) butter
1 onion, peeled and finely sliced
200g (7oz) rindless unsmoked bacon (preferably
   in one piece), cut into 0.5 x 2cm (¼ x ¾in) pieces
50g (2oz) plain flour
200g (7oz) frozen peas
2 tbsp chopped parsley
Salt and freshly ground black pepper
1kg (2lb 3oz) mashed potato (see page 199)

Equipment
20 x 30cm (8 x 12in) ovenproof dish

Bring a small saucepan of water to a rolling boil and carefully lower in the eggs using a slotted spoon. Bring back up to the boil and cook the eggs for 8 minutes to hard-boil them. Remove from the pan and rinse under cold water for a few seconds, then peel off the shells and cut the eggs into quarters lengthways.

Meanwhile, pour the milk into a wide, shallow saucepan and place on a medium heat. When the milk is simmering, add the smoked haddock and poach for 2–3 minutes or until just cooked. Remove from the heat, then drain the fish, reserving the milk to use later. Peel the skin

from the fish and remove any bones, then break the flesh into large flakes and place in a bowl.

Preheat the oven to 200°C (400°F), Gas mark 6.

Melt the butter in a separate, large saucepan on a medium heat. When the butter is foaming, add the onion and bacon pieces. Fry, stirring occasionally, for 8–10 minutes or until the onion is soft and lightly browned. Add the flour and continue cooking for another 2 minutes or so, stirring frequently. Pour in the reserved milk and stir frequently as you bring to the boil, using a whisk to get rid of any lumps of flour, then remove from the heat.

Stir in the peas and chopped parsley, then gently fold in the boiled eggs and fish and season with salt and pepper to taste (bearing in mind that the smoked haddock and bacon are salty already). Tip into the ovenproof dish, then add the mashed potato in blobs and gently spread it out to cover the fish mixture. Bake for 30 minutes or until golden on top and bubbling, then remove from the oven and serve.

✳ This can be made ahead (up until covering in the mashed potato) and stored, unbaked, in the fridge for up to 24 hours.

Although the pie is best eaten straight after cooking, it will keep in the fridge for up to 24 hours. Reheat in a moderate oven (preheated to 180°C/350°F/Gas mark 4) for about 10 minutes to serve.

INSTANT CULLEN SKINK

Assertive, smoky and bolder in flavour than a chowder or bisque, Cullen skink is the defining Scottish soup. The name comes from Cullen, a town in northeast Scotland, and skink, a Scots word for 'shin of beef' that then evolved into 'soup' as this was frequently made with beef shin. Packed with flavour yet so simple to make, it is one of my favourite ways of using leftover mashed potato.

Serves 6–8

800ml (1 pint 9fl oz) double or regular cream

800ml (1 pint 9fl oz) milk

400g (14oz) smoked haddock fillets (preferably undyed)

400g (14oz) mashed potato (see page 199)

Salt and freshly ground black pepper

2 tbsp chopped chives

Pour the cream and milk into a large saucepan and add the haddock. Place on a medium heat and bring to a simmer, then cook for 5–10 minutes or until the fish is flaky.

Place the mashed potato in a separate pan and heat gently to warm through. Divide the mashed potato between individual bowls, then use a slotted spoon to lift the fish out of the hot cream and milk. Remove the skin and any bones from the cooked fish, then divide into portions and place on top of the mashed potato.

Taste the hot cream, adding salt and pepper if needed, then pour it over the fish and potato. Scatter the chives on top and serve immediately.

⊝ The quantities in this recipe can be halved or multiplied.

FISH GRATIN WITH CRUNCHY, CHEESY BREADCRUMBS

I adore this rich gratin, the white fish coated in a thick cheese sauce and topped with crisp buttery breadcrumbs. You could use haddock or cod, but pollock or ling are equally good and less expensive too.

Serves 6

15g (½oz) butter

2 leeks, trimmed and thinly sliced (125g/4½oz sliced weight)

600g (1lb 2oz) skinned fillets of white fish, such as cod, haddock, whiting, pollock or ling, each cut into 6 portions (see tip below)

For the Mornay sauce

35g (1¼oz) butter

35g (1¼oz) plain flour

500ml (18fl oz) milk

175g (6oz) Cheddar or Gruyère cheese, grated

1 tsp Dijon mustard

Salt and freshly ground black pepper

For the cheesy breadcrumbs

25g (1oz) butter

50g (2oz) breadcrumbs

25g (1oz) Cheddar or Gruyère cheese, grated

Equipment

20 x 30cm (8 x 12in) ovenproof dish or 6 individual dishes

First make the Mornay sauce. Melt the butter in a saucepan on a medium heat, then add the flour and whisk for 1 minute. Remove from the heat and gradually add the milk, whisking all the time to remove any lumps. Place the pan back over the heat and bring to the boil, whisking the sauce while it thickens (which it will do once it comes to a rolling boil). Remove from the heat and allow to cool for 1 minute before whisking in the grated cheese and the mustard. Season with salt and pepper to taste and set aside.

To cook the leeks, melt the 15g (½oz) of butter in a separate saucepan on a medium heat. When the butter is foaming, add the leeks and season with salt and pepper. Turn the heat down to low and cover the pan with a lid. Cook for 2–3 minutes, tossing once or twice, or until the leeks are wilted but still bright green.

Make the cheesy breadcrumbs by first melting the 25g (1oz) of butter in another saucepan. Remove the pan from the heat and stir in the breadcrumbs and grated cheese.

Preheat the oven to 180°C (350°F), Gas mark 4. To assemble the gratin, tip the leeks into the

RACHEL'S TIPS If using the tail end of the fish, it's a good idea to fold the thinner end under (in half) so that this portion is the same thickness as the other pieces and therefore cooks at the same rate.

For a more traditional presentation, you can pipe mashed potato (see page 199) – using a piping bag with a star-shaped nozzle – around the sides of the dish before it goes into the oven.

large ovenproof dish or divide between the six individual dishes. Place the fish portions on top of the leeks, then cover with the Mornay sauce and scatter the cheesy breadcrumbs over the top.

Place in the oven and cook for 30–40 minutes for the single large dish or 18–20 minutes for the individual dishes. The breadcrumbs should be golden and the sauce bubbling hot. To check that the gratin is cooked through, insert a metal skewer into the centre of a piece of fish. Leave it in for 10 seconds, then remove it – the skewer should be too hot to hold on the inside of your wrist.

This dish is delicious served with mashed potato (see page 199) and perhaps a salad.

✳ This can be made ahead, up to the point of assembling the dish prior to baking, and stored in the fridge overnight, but make sure the leeks and Mornay sauce have cooled down first. It can also be frozen for up to three months, if kept well covered. Allow to defrost completely before baking as above.

⬠ Any leftover gratin can be made into fishcakes (see page 69).

FISHCAKES

These fishcakes are ideal for using up any leftover fish gratin (see page 66), the rich flavour of that dish given a little lift with fresh herbs and added texture from the lovely crisp coating. My boys like these even more than the original gratin!

Makes 4 fishcakes

500g (1lb 2oz) Fish Gratin with Crunchy, Cheesy
  Breadcrumbs (see page 66) (see ⊖ below)
1 tbsp finely chopped tarragon or dill
4 tbsp plain flour
Salt and freshly ground black pepper
1 egg
75g (3oz) fresh white breadcrumbs
2 tbsp olive oil
25g (1oz) butter

Place the fish gratin in a large bowl, add the herbs and stir together well. Using your hands, shape the mixture into fishcakes about 6cm (2½in) wide and 1.5cm (⅝in) thick.

Sprinkle the flour onto a plate and season with salt and pepper. Crack the egg into a bowl and beat well, then place the bowl next to the seasoned flour. Spread the breadcrumbs out on another plate.

Dip a fishcake into the seasoned flour, then into the beaten egg and then into the breadcrumbs, making sure it is completely coated in all three ingredients. Place on a clean plate and repeat with the rest of the fishcakes.

Place the olive oil and butter in a large frying pan on a medium heat. When the butter has melted, add the fishcakes and fry on each side for about 4–6 minutes or until golden and crisp. Place on kitchen paper to drain, then repeat with any remaining fishcakes, adding more olive oil as necessary. Serve with mayonnaise, green salad leaves and a slice of lemon.

✳ The fishcakes can be made up to the point of coating them in breadcrumbs. They will keep in the fridge for a few hours before being fried as above.

⊖ The quantities given above are based on a particular amount of fish gratin, but use however much you have left over (even if it means you can make only one fishcake!) and alter the quantities of the other ingredients accordingly. Depending on how many you're cooking, you may need to fry them in more than one batch too.

MUSSELS COOKED IN CIDER

We frequently cook with wine but rarely turn to cider, yet it goes so well in certain recipes. Paired with mussels and bacon, as here, it makes for a really delicious dish. This is also such a good way to cook mussels – still the most affordable type of seafood and one of my favourites too. The rich and creamy juices demand thick chunks of crusty bread for thorough mopping up!

Serves 4

2.5kg (5½lb) fresh mussels
15g (½oz) butter
1 onion, peeled and finely chopped
3 cloves of garlic, peeled and crushed
    or finely grated
6 rashers of rindless streaky bacon, cut into
    0.5 x 2cm (¼ x ¾in) pieces
400ml (14fl oz) dry cider
100ml (3½fl oz) double or regular cream
1 tbsp finely chopped parsley
1 tbsp finely chopped chives
Salt and freshly ground black pepper

Scrub the mussels thoroughly and remove any beards (fibrous tufts). Discard any with open shells that do not close when sharply tapped against a hard surface.

Place a large saucepan or casserole dish – big enough to hold all the mussels – on a medium heat. Add the butter and, when melted, add the onion, garlic and bacon and cook gently for 6–8 minutes or until the onion is softened.

Pour in the cider and bring to a simmer. Allow to simmer for 1 minute, then add the mussels and cover with a tight-fitting lid. Increase the heat to high and cook for 3–4 minutes, stirring occasionally, until all the mussels have opened. Discard any that do not.

Drain the mussels in a colander, reserving the cooking liquid, then return the mussels to the pan to keep warm. Pour the cooking juices through a sieve into another pan, add the cream and herbs and bring to the boil, seasoning with salt and pepper to taste.

Divide the mussels between individual bowls and pour over the hot sauce, then serve immediately with chunks of crusty bread.

⊖ You can halve the quantities, if you wish, or double them if you have a large enough pot.

SAFFRON CLAMS

This dish takes its inspiration from Spain, where it can be found on tapas menus all over the southern coast. The clams are cooked with the lid on so that they steam in the pan, releasing gorgeous juices that then mix with the other ingredients to create a wonderful sauce for which the best accompaniment is crusty bread.

Serves 4–6 as tapas, or 2 as a main course
1kg (2lb 3oz) fresh clams
3 tbsp olive oil
1 small onion, peeled and finely chopped
1 clove of garlic, peeled and finely chopped
Pinch of saffron threads
¼ tsp smoked paprika
50ml (2fl oz) dry sherry, such as fino
1 tbsp tomato paste
2 tbsp roughly chopped parsley

First check that the clams are all closed, discarding any that stay open when tapped on a hard surface. To clean the clams, place them in a bowl or sink of cold water and let them soak for 30 minutes; this should help get rid of any sand. Drain the clams and set aside.

Heat the olive oil in a wide saucepan over a medium heat, then add the onion and sauté for about 5 minutes or until softened and golden. Add the remaining ingredients and the drained clams, cover with a lid and cook for 3–4 minutes or until all the clams have completely opened. Discard any that have not.

Tip into serving bowls and serve immediately, mopping up the juices with chunks of crusty white bread.

⊖ The quantities in this recipe can be halved or multiplied, depending on how many you're feeding.

MEXICAN-STYLE PRAWNS WITH GUACAMOLE AND TOMATO SALSA

✳ ⌂

I love to use locally caught prawns for this recipe. In Ireland they're called Dublin Bay prawns, or just prawns; in the UK they're known as langoustines. Don't discard the shells (see ⌂). They are the key ingredient in the divine prawn bisque on p77.

Serves 4–6

4 large wheat or corn tortillas, each cut into 8 wedges
3 tbsp olive oil, plus extra for drizzling
Sea salt and freshly ground black pepper
500g (1lb 2oz) raw shell-on prawns, or about 400g (14oz) raw peeled prawns
3 large cloves of garlic, peeled and finely chopped
1–2 fresh red chilli peppers, deseeded (optional) and finely chopped

For the guacamole

2 ripe avocados, peeled, destoned and flesh mashed
2 tbsp chopped coriander
1 large clove of garlic, peeled and crushed or finely grated
½ fresh red chilli pepper, deseeded (optional) and finely chopped
2 tbsp lime or lemon juice
2 tbsp olive oil

For the tomato salsa

200g (7oz) cherry tomatoes, quartered, or large ripe tomatoes, cut into 1cm (½in) chunks
½ red onion, peeled and finely chopped
¼–½ cucumber, finely chopped
Good squeeze of lime or lemon juice
2 tbsp chopped coriander

To serve

2 tbsp chopped coriander
Lime wedges
Sour cream

Preheat the oven to 220°C (475°F), Gas mark 7.

Lay out the tortilla wedges in single layers on baking sheets, drizzle with olive oil, sprinkle with salt and heat in the oven for 5–7 minutes or until light golden. Remove from the oven and set aside.

Meanwhile, mix together the guacamole ingredients in a bowl, seasoning to taste.

In a separate bowl, mix together the tomato salsa ingredients, seasoning to taste.

Next cook the prawns. Place a large frying pan or wok on a high heat. When the pan is hot, add the olive oil. If you're using peeled prawns, add the garlic and chilli first, stir-fry for 30–60 seconds or until the garlic is lightly golden, then add the prawns and a pinch of salt. Toss over the heat for 1–2 minutes or until the prawns are opaque and cooked through. If using prawns in their shells, put these in the pan after adding the oil and stir-fry for 3–4 minutes or until the shells turn lightly golden, then add the garlic, chilli and a pinch of salt. Stir-fry until the prawns are cooked through and the garlic is golden. Tip the prawns into a serving dish and scatter with the coriander.

Put the guacamole, salsa and tortilla wedges in the centre of the table with the hot prawns, lime wedges and a bowl of sour cream, then dig in!

✳ The salsa can be made ahead but should be eaten within a few hours for it to be at its best. If chilling, take it out of the fridge about 30 minutes before serving so it can come up to room temperature.

The guacamole can also be prepared a few hours in advance, providing its surface is covered with cling film to stop it going brown. If you're chilling it take it out about 30 minutes before serving to bring it up to room temperature.

⌂ Store leftover prawn shells in the freezer to make prawn bisque (see page 77).

PRAWN BISQUE WITH GARLIC MAYONNAISE CROUTONS

What's wonderful about this soup is that something that tastes so luxurious can be made so economically, using what would otherwise be discarded langoustine (Dublin Bay prawn) heads, claws and shells (see Mexican-style Prawns on page 74). Small prawns or shrimps can also be used. At home we love to serve this as a family evening meal.

Serves 4–6

25g (1oz) butter

150g (5oz) shallots, peeled and finely chopped

2 cloves of garlic, peeled and crushed
   or finely grated

Salt and freshly ground black pepper

450g (1lb) heads, claws and tail shells from
   langoustines/Dublin Bay prawns or small
   prawns/shrimps (left over from making the
   Mexican-style Prawns – see page 74)

2 x 400g tins of chopped tomatoes or 800g
   (1¾lb) ripe tomatoes, chopped

400ml (14fl oz) fish or light chicken stock
   (see page 20)

1 tsp sugar

200ml (7fl oz) double or regular cream

2 tbsp brandy (optional but enriches the flavour)

1 tbsp chopped parsley

For the garlic mayonnaise croutons

75g (3oz) mayonnaise

1 clove of garlic, peeled and crushed
   or finely grated

12 slices of baguette

Melt the butter in a saucepan on a medium heat until foaming, then add the shallots and garlic. Season with salt and pepper and cover, then reduce the heat and sweat the shallots for 7–8 minutes.

While the shallots are cooking, use a rolling pin to crush and bash the langoustine/prawn heads and shells to smaller pieces. They don't need to be too small but the more you break them up, the more flavour you'll extract.

Once the shallots have softened, add the crushed langoustine/prawn heads and shells to the pan. Turn up the heat to medium and cook, uncovered and stirring regularly, for 6–8 minutes or until you can smell the shells beginning to toast and see them turning light golden in colour.

Add the tomatoes, stock and sugar and cook over a high heat for 10 minutes or until the tomatoes have softened completely. Pour into a blender or food processor and whiz for a few minutes to break the shells.

Meanwhile, prepare the croutons. Mix the mayonnaise and garlic in a bowl and toast the bread on both sides.

Pour the puréed langoustine/prawn shell mixture through a sieve into a clean saucepan and place on a medium heat. Add the cream and brandy (if using), season with salt and pepper to taste and cook the bisque gently to heat through. (You may need to add a pinch more sugar if using tinned tomatoes.) Sprinkle with the parsley and serve immediately with pieces of toast spread with the garlic mayonnaise spread.

✳ The bisque can be made ahead and stored in the fridge for up to 24 hours. It can also be frozen for up to three months.

PRAWN AND ASPARAGUS SPAGHETTI

I adore this sort of dish, which uses a short list of great ingredients to make something special. The crème fraîche is flavoured by the prawns as it cooks them to make a silken sauce for the spaghetti. So simple to make and so quick, but still a sublime and luxurious meal.

Serves 4–6

Salt and freshly ground black pepper

300g (11oz) spaghetti or other pasta, such as fettuccine, linguine or tagliatelle

150g (5oz) stalks of asparagus, woody ends snapped off and discarded, spears cut at an angle into roughly 4cm (1½in) lengths

250g (9oz) crème fraîche

15–20 large raw peeled prawns, halved lengthways

Juice of 1 lemon

2 tbsp chopped parsley

Place a large saucepan of salted water on a high heat and bring to the boil. Once the water is boiling, add the spaghetti and cook for the length of time specified in the packet instructions or until al dente, adding the asparagus pieces 2–3 minutes before the end of the cooking time. Drain the spaghetti and asparagus in a colander, retaining 50ml (2fl oz) of the cooking liquid, then return the spaghetti and asparagus to the pan with the reserved liquid.

Spoon the crème fraîche into another large saucepan and place on a medium heat. When the crème fraîche is hot, add the prawns, season with salt and pepper and heat for 1–2 minutes or until the prawns are just cooked.

Add the spaghetti and asparagus to the pan, followed by the lemon juice and chopped parsley. Stir together and taste for seasoning, adding more lemon juice if necessary, then serve immediately.

POULTRY

ROAST CHICKEN WITH WHITE WINE, LEEKS AND CARROTS

This is the sort of dish I make the most at home; I love the convenience of throwing everything into the same roasting tin. This particular recipe also makes for a magical melding of flavours – the wine and chicken juices mixing with the vegetables so that each enhances the other. The perfect one-pot dish!

Serves 4–6
1 x 1.5–2.25kg (3lb 5oz–5lb) chicken
1 lemon, quartered
6 unpeeled cloves of garlic, halved
1 small onion, peeled and halved
4 large sprigs of thyme
Salt and freshly ground black pepper
250ml (9fl oz) white wine
400g (14oz) unpeeled new potatoes, halved
  or quartered
25g (1oz) butter
6 carrots, peeled and cut at an angle into
  2cm (¾in) slices
2 leeks, trimmed and cut at an angle into
  2cm (¾in) slices
50ml (2fl oz) olive oil
100ml (3½fl oz) chicken stock (see page 20)

Preheat the oven to 180°C (350°F), Gas mark 4.

Stuff the chicken with the lemon, garlic, onion and thyme, then place in a large, deep-sided roasting tin and season all over with salt and pepper. Pour the wine into the bottom of the roasting tin, then cover the chicken and tin tightly with foil. Place in the oven and roast

for 30–45 minutes, depending on the size of your chicken.

Take the chicken out of the oven, remove the foil and add the potatoes to the tin, seasoning them with salt and pepper. Cover again with foil and return to the oven to roast for another 30 minutes.

Remove from the oven, take off the foil and spread the butter all over the chicken. Add the carrots and leeks to the tin, drizzling with the olive oil and seasoning with salt and pepper, then return to the oven for a further 30 minutes or until the vegetables are tender and the chicken golden on top and cooked through (see tips below).

Remove from the oven, transfer the chicken to a warmed plate and wrap in foil to keep warm. Tip the juices from the roasting tin into a separating jug or, if you don't have one, pour them into a bowl and add a few ice cubes, then leave to stand for about 5 minutes or until the fat rises to the top. Spoon off the fat, then pour the juices into a saucepan with the chicken stock and bring to the boil. Season with salt and pepper to taste and serve with the chicken and vegetables.

RACHEL'S TIPS If the chicken is getting quite brown during cooking, cover again with foil for the rest of the cooking time.

To check that the chicken is cooked, pierce one of the thighs with a skewer: if the juices run clear, then the meat is done; if they are still pink, the chicken will need cooking for a bit longer. Likewise, if you gently pull on one of the legs and it feels as though it will come away quite easily, this shows that the chicken is ready to come out of the oven.

✳ This recipe is quick and easy to make, but if you like you could have the chicken stuffed and ready to roast – it would keep, wrapped in foil or cling film, in the fridge for up to two days. You could prepare all the vegetables ahead of time, too (keeping the potatoes in a bowl of water so that they don't go brown), ready to add to the roasting tin while the chicken is roasting.

The cooked chicken will keep, covered, in the fridge for two days.

⊖⊕ If you'd like to serve just two people, you could use four chicken thighs or two breasts and halve the quantities of the other ingredients.

And rather than using them to stuff the chicken, you could place the lemon, garlic, onion and thyme in the roasting tin with the chicken pieces on top. Or you could just cook the whole chicken and have lots of delicious leftovers!

⊡ The leftover chicken would of course be delicious in salads or sandwiches. It would also be perfect in the Quick Chicken Casserole (see page 86), Chicken and Ham Pie (see page 89), or Chicken, Fennel and Orange Salad (see page 98). (You could use any leftover gravy in the pie too.)

Reserve the chicken carcass for making stock (see page 20).

QUICK CHICKEN CASSEROLE

This is a smart and speedy way of transforming leftover roast chicken into a completely new dish. To accompany all that sweet and creamy sauce, I love to serve mashed potato (see page 199), pilaf rice (see page 190) or even just plain boiled rice. You can leave out the cream entirely, if you prefer.

Serves 4

2 tbsp olive oil

15g (½oz) butter

2 large shallots, peeled and chopped

250g (9oz) button mushrooms, sliced

125ml (4½fl oz) white wine

1 x 400g tin of chopped tomatoes or 400g (14oz) ripe tomatoes, peeled (see tip on p58) and chopped

1 tbsp tomato paste or purée

1 tsp sugar

2 large sprigs of tarragon and 2 tbsp chopped tarragon for sprinkling

Salt and freshly ground black pepper

400g (14oz) raw or cooked chicken (see page 82), cut into roughly 1 x 2cm (½ x ¾in) pieces

100ml (3½fl oz) double or regular cream

Place a wide frying pan or medium-sized saucepan (see tip below) on a medium heat. Add the olive oil and butter and when the butter has melted, add the shallots and mushrooms. Sauté, stirring occasionally, for 5–10 minutes or until soft and lightly browned.

Add the wine with the tomatoes, tomato paste or purée, sugar and sprigs of tarragon. Season with salt and pepper, then bring to the boil. Reduce the heat and simmer for 15 minutes.

Add the raw chicken (if using) and the cream, then bring back up to a simmer and continue to simmer for 10 minutes or until the chicken is cooked through. If using cooked chicken, simmer for 5 minutes or until heated through. Remove the tarragon sprigs, then sprinkle over the chopped tarragon and serve.

(✻) This will keep happily in the fridge for up to three days, but if you do plan on making it ahead, then still add the chopped tarragon just before serving.

(-+) This recipe could easily be halved if cooking for fewer people, or if you have a large enough pot you could multiply the quantities.

RACHEL'S TIP It's important to use a wide enough pan that when you cook the shallots and mushrooms they go brown. If the pot is too small, they won't brown properly and you'll lose some of that lovely flavour.

CHICKEN AND HAM PIE

A pie is just the thing to warm up a cold winter's day, when freezing rain is battering at the windows. It's such a fantastic way of using cooked chicken and ham, too, not to mention other leftovers. While I usually make this recipe with chicken, you can of course use turkey instead.

Serves 6–8

25g (1oz) butter

1 onion, peeled and finely chopped

400g (14oz) broccoli florets, or leftover boiled or Roasted Broccoli (see page 204)

Salt and freshly ground black pepper

25g (1oz) plain flour

225ml (8fl oz) double or regular cream

225ml (8fl oz) chicken stock (see page 20) or leftover gravy (see page 82)

675g (1½lb) cooked chicken (see page 82) and ham (see page 171), cut into 2cm (¾in) chunks

1 tbsp chopped tarragon or marjoram

1kg (2lb 3oz) mashed potato (see page 199)

Equipment

20 x 30cm (8 x 12in) ovenproof dish

Preheat the oven to 180°C (350°F), Gas mark 4.

Melt the butter in a large saucepan on a medium heat, add the onion and fry gently for 8–10 minutes or until completely soft and a little golden around the edges.

Meanwhile, if using raw broccoli, place a saucepan of water on a high heat and add a good pinch of salt. When the water comes to the boil, drop in the broccoli florets and cover with a lid, keeping the pan covered until the water comes back up to the boil. As soon as it begins to boil, remove the lid and cook the broccoli for 2–4 minutes or until just tender – it should still have a little bite to it. Drain the broccoli and set aside.

Add the flour to the onion and, using a whisk to mix it in, cook for 1 minute, then pour in the cream and stock (or gravy), whisking all the while to mix them in. Bring to the boil, then reduce the heat and simmer for 1–2 minutes or until the sauce has thickened a little.

Stir in the chicken, ham, chopped herbs and the freshly cooked (or leftover) broccoli, then season to taste with salt and pepper. Pour into the ovenproof dish and top with the mashed potato, spooning it on in dollops and spreading with a fork.

Bake in the oven for 25–30 minutes or until golden brown on top and bubbling hot.

⊘ **Turkey and ham pie:** Instead of leftover chicken, you could use turkey – an ideal way of using up all the leftover turkey (and ham) at Christmas, in fact. You could also boil up the turkey carcass to make stock (as you would for chicken stock – see page 20) and use that instead of the chicken stock, if you preferred.

✳ This can be prepared in advance up to the point of cooking it in the oven, and kept, covered, in the fridge for up to two days. It can also be frozen.

ROSEMARY AND GARLIC SPATCHCOCK CHICKEN WITH BULGUR WHEAT SALAD

Bulgur wheat does a great job of soaking up the chicken juices in this dish, while the jewel-like pomegranate seeds add a gorgeous sweet-sour flavour. Any leftover chicken and salad could simply be mixed together for a divine packed lunch the following day.

Serves 4–6
1 x 1.5–2.25kg (3lb 5oz–5lb) chicken

For the marinade
50ml (2fl oz) olive oil
Juice and finely grated zest of 1 lemon
4 cloves of garlic, peeled and crushed or
    finely grated
2 tbsp chopped rosemary leaves
Salt and freshly ground black pepper

For the salad
200g (7oz) bulgur wheat
Juice and finely grated zest of 1 lemon
Seeds and juice of 1 pomegranate (see tip below)
1 tbsp chopped mint
1 tbsp chopped parsley
50ml (2fl oz) olive oil

First prepare the chicken. To remove the backbone, use very sharp scissors to cut through the chicken on both sides of the bone all the way from the top to the bottom. Remove the backbone and open the chicken out like a book, then place the chicken, breast side up, on your worktop and use the palms of your hands to flatten it. Using a sharp knife, make a few slashes in the legs.

To make the marinade, place all the ingredients in a bowl, season with salt and pepper and mix together. (If marinating the chicken overnight, don't add salt until the next day as it will draw the moisture out of the meat.)

Place the chicken in a wide, shallow dish and pour over the marinade, making sure it gets into every crevice, including the cuts in the legs. Cover with cling film and place in the fridge to chill for at least 2 hours or even overnight.

When you are ready to cook the chicken, preheat the oven to 220°C (425°F), Gas mark 7.

Place the marinated chicken in a roasting tin with all the marinade and bake in the oven for 1–1½ hours (the cooking time will vary greatly depending on the size of the chicken) until cooked (see tip on page 82).

While the chicken is cooking, make the salad. Cover the bulgur wheat in boiling water and leave to soak for 10–15 minutes or until just soft, then drain.

In a bowl, mix the lemon juice and zest with the pomegranate seeds and juice, herbs and olive oil. Stir in the bulgur wheat and season to taste.

When the chicken is cooked, cover with foil, while still in the tin, and leave to rest somewhere

RACHEL'S TIP This smart trick for removing the seeds of a pomegranate avoids fiddly peeling and excess pith. Cut the pomegranate in half, then hold one half over a large bowl, cut side down, in the palm of your cupped hand. Using the back of a wooden spoon, hit the pomegranate; the seeds will pop out and fall through your fingers into the bowl. Keep hitting the back of the pomegranate and you'll soon have a bowl full of seeds. Remove any bits of pith, then repeat with the other half.

warm – such as in the oven, with the heat switched off – for a few minutes, then carve into pieces and serve with the bulgur wheat salad.

✳ Leftover meat will keep for a couple of days after cooking, if chilled. You could serve the salad with previously cooked or leftover chicken, too.

The bulgur wheat salad can be made a few hours ahead, though keep it covered so that it doesn't dry out.

⊖⊕ You could cook one or two small chickens to feed fewer or more people.

The quantities for the bulgur wheat salad can be halved for fewer people or multiplied for a crowd.

🗓 Leftovers would be perfect for a packed lunch or to use in the Quick Chicken Casserole (see page 86).

You could use the carcass to make chicken stock (see page 20).

ROAST CHICKEN PIECES WITH LEMON AND HERB AÏOLI

To save time, I sometimes roast a jointed chicken instead of a whole bird as it cooks much faster. The real point of this dish, though, is the sauce! Punchy and strong-tasting, the lemon and herb aïoli would work well in sandwiches or in salads, but here it is mixed with the chicken juices to make the most delicious sauce. Serve warm, as soon as it's made, or at room temperature. The sauce would also be wonderful with a whole roast chicken.

Serves 4–6

1 x 1.5–2.25kg (3lb 5oz–5lb) chicken, jointed
  into drumsticks, thighs, breasts and wings
  (ask your butcher to do this for you)
4 large shallots or 2 red onions, peeled and
  quartered through the root
8 potatoes, peeled, and halved or quartered
  if large
½ tbsp finely chopped rosemary
½ tsp chopped thyme
25ml (1fl oz) olive oil
Salt and freshly ground black pepper

For the lemon and herb aïoli

2–4 cloves of garlic, peeled and crushed
  or finely grated
2 egg yolks (see ⬜ opposite)
1 tbsp lemon juice
1 generous tsp Dijon mustard
½ tbsp finely chopped rosemary leaves
½ tsp chopped thyme leaves
175ml (6fl oz) sunflower oil
50ml (2fl oz) olive oil
100ml (3½fl oz) chicken stock (see page 20)
  or water

Preheat the oven to 220°C (425°F), Gas mark 7.

Place the chicken pieces, skin side up, in a roasting tin and add the shallots or onions, potatoes and herbs. Drizzle over the olive oil and season generously with salt and pepper, then roast in the oven for 25–35 minutes or until the chicken is cooked (see tip on page 82) and browned on top and the potatoes and onions are tender and lightly golden.

Meanwhile, make the aïoli. Place the garlic in a bowl with the egg yolks, lemon juice, mustard, herbs and a pinch of salt. Put the sunflower and olive oil in a jug and slowly pour into the egg yolk mixture in a very thin stream while whisking constantly, either by hand or using a hand-held electric beater. Continue to add the oil, whisking all the time, until it is fully incorporated and the mixture has thickened. Taste and add more salt and lemon juice, if necessary.

Once the chicken is cooked, remove from the oven, then transfer the chicken and vegetable pieces to a warmed serving dish and cover with foil to keep warm.

Place the roasting tin on the hob on a medium heat, pour in the stock (or water) and use a whisk to help break up and dissolve the caramelised chicken juices sticking to the bottom of the tin. Bring to the boil, then tip into a jug and leave to sit for a couple of minutes to allow the fat to float to the top. (You could add a few ice cubes, if you liked, to help speed up the process.) Spoon off the fat and reheat the liquid in a saucepan if it has cooled down completely.

Slowly pour the liquid into the aïoli while whisking constantly. This is your sauce to serve with the chicken and potatoes. Don't try to reheat it at this stage as it will split, but it is just as good served at room temperature.

You can make the aïoli ahead as it will keep happily in the fridge for up to five days.

The cooked chicken will keep in the fridge for a couple of days.

The quantities in this recipe can be halved to serve 2–3, using two chicken thighs or one breast per person rather than a whole chicken. Equally, if you'd like to serve more than six people, the quantities can easily be multiplied.

Keep the leftover egg whites for making meringues (see page 257) or pavlova.

CHICKEN LIVERS WITH SHERRY

This recipe was inspired by a trip to the Spanish city of Jerez de la Frontera, the home of sherry. I love to drink dry sherry as an aperitif, but it also brings its unique taste to a number of Spanish dishes, including this one. Serve tapas-style with crusty bread for a few people, or on buttered toast as lunch for two. Simple but so delicious!

Serves 2–3 as a snack or light lunch
2 tbsp olive oil
1 clove of garlic, peeled and sliced
300g (11oz) chicken livers, any
   membrane removed
Salt and freshly ground black pepper
75ml (3fl oz) dry sherry, such as fino
   or manzanilla
1–2 tbsp chopped parsley

Pour the olive oil into a frying pan and place on a medium heat. When hot add the garlic and the chicken livers, season with salt and pepper and cook the livers for 2–3 minutes on each side or until they're browned on the outside but still a little pink in the middle.

Add the sherry, increase the heat and allow to bubble for 1–2 minutes, then remove from the heat and stir in the parsley. Serve immediately with some crusty bread to mop up all the juices.

The quantities in this recipe can be halved or multiplied.

CHICKEN AND BACON CASSEROLE

✳ ⊕ ⊟

**Brandy is the not-so-secret ingredient in so many different recipes. It has a unique
intensity that really comes through in soups, stews and of course flambéed dishes!
The recipe below uses quite a large amount, but the alcohol mostly evaporates during
cooking, leaving only the pure, concentrated flavour. This casserole makes the most
of just a few ingredients, the brandy and cream adding a luxurious yet comforting
touch. I like to serve it with some simple boiled or mashed potatoes (see page 199)
or even pilaf rice (see page 190).**

Serves 4–6

1 x 1.5–2.25kg (3lb 5oz–5lb) chicken, jointed
 into drumsticks, thighs, breasts and wings
 (ask your butcher to do this for you)
Salt and freshly ground black pepper
2 tbsp olive oil
300g (11oz) rindless streaky bacon (preferably
 in one piece), cut into 1cm (½in) chunks
2 leeks, trimmed and sliced at an angle
 into 1.5cm (⅝in) pieces (350g/12oz
 trimmed weight)
150ml (5fl oz) brandy
150ml (5fl oz) chicken stock (see page 20)
2 sprigs of thyme and 2 tsp chopped thyme leaves
200ml (7fl oz) double or regular cream

Preheat the oven (if not cooking the dish on the
hob) to 150°C (300°F), Gas mark 2.

Place a large saucepan or casserole dish on a
medium–high heat and allow to get hot. Season
the skin side of the chicken pieces with salt and
pepper, then pour the olive oil into the pot and
add the chicken pieces, skin side down. Season
the other side of the chicken with salt and pepper
and cook for 3–4 minutes on each side or until
the pieces are golden all over. Remove the
chicken pieces from the pot (keeping it on the
heat) and set aside.

Add the bacon and toss in the pan or dish for
4–5 minutes or until golden, then tip in the leeks
and sauté for another minute before adding the

brandy and stock, the browned chicken pieces
and the sprigs of thyme. Bring to a gentle boil,
then cover with a lid, turn the heat down to very
low and leave to simmer on the hob or cook in
the oven (if using) for 20–30 minutes or until
the chicken is cooked (the flesh white all the
way through).

Transfer the chicken, bacon and leeks to a
large bowl, discarding the sprigs of thyme, and
cover with a plate or saucepan lid to keep warm.

Pour the cream into the juices in the pot and
boil for 4–5 minutes, uncovered, until slightly
thickened. Add the chopped thyme and season
to taste with salt and pepper, then tip the chicken,
leeks, bacon and any juices into the sauce. Heat
through for a minute or so, stirring regularly, and
serve immediately.

✳ Although best eaten on the day, this dish will
keep really well in the fridge for up to 48 hours.
Simply place back on the hob (having transferred
the mixture to a large saucepan) and simmer for
a few minutes before serving.

⊕ To serve 2–3 people, the quantities in this
recipe could be halved, using 4–6 chicken thighs
or 2–3 breasts (two thighs or one breast per
person) instead of the jointed chicken pieces.

⊟ Reserve any leftover bones to make chicken
stock (see page 20).

CHICKEN, FENNEL AND ORANGE SALAD

Crisp, crunchy fennel and sweet juicy oranges make for a seriously summery roast chicken. Roast chicken needn't always be surrounded by an assortment of roast vegetables, sometimes the warm moist meat demands to be part of a salad – especially when the sun is shining. Of course you could also use leftover roast chicken in this salad which would be very good as well.

Serves 4–6
1 x 1.5–2.25kg (3lb 5oz–5lb) chicken
2 tbsp olive oil
Salt and freshly ground black pepper

For the fennel and orange salad
2 oranges
2 fennel bulbs
2 tbsp finely chopped parsley
Juice and finely grated zest of ½ lemon
2 tbsp olive oil
4 large handfuls of salad leaves

Preheat the oven to 180°C (350°F), Gas mark 4.

Put the chicken in a roasting tin, drizzle over the olive oil and sprinkle with salt and pepper. Place in the oven and roast for 1½–1¾ hours or until cooked through (see tip on page 82).

While the chicken is cooking, you can start preparing the salad. First peel and segment each orange. Using a small, sharp knife and working over a bowl to catch the juices, cut off the ends, then carefully cut away the peel and pith in a spiral until you have a peeled orange with only flesh and no pith. Next carefully cut along the edge of each segment, leaving behind the membrane and freeing a wedge of flesh from the pith. Repeat for all the segments and place the flesh in the bowl; squeeze the peel and remaining membrane into the bowl to catch any extra juice,

then discard. Instead of segmenting the oranges, you can if you wish cut each peeled orange horizontally to make round slices.

To prepare the fennel, slice off the fronds (the feathery bits on top) and reserve these for using later. Cut off the stalks and discard, then cut the bulb into slices 5mm (¼in) thick.

When the chicken is cooked, allow to rest somewhere warm (such in as the oven, with the heat switched off) for 5 minutes, then carve into pieces and tear or cut these into roughly bite-sized chunks. Place in a large bowl with the fennel slices, orange segments and any juices, chopped parsley, lemon juice and zest and the olive oil. Toss together gently and season with salt and pepper.

Drain off a little of the liquid from the dish and use to dress the salad leaves in a separate bowl, then place the leaves in the middle of a large serving plate. Tip the chicken mixture around the salad, then scatter over the reserved fennel fronds to serve.

(✳) Though the chicken is wonderful in this recipe if freshly roasted and still a little warm, you could also use chicken that you've previously roasted. It will keep, covered, in the fridge for a couple of days. The salad can't be made ahead, however.

RACHEL'S TIP If the chicken is getting quite brown during cooking, cover with foil for the rest of the cooking time.

You could halve the quantities in this recipe, using 4–6 chicken thighs or 2–3 breasts (two thighs or one breast per person) rather than a whole chicken, and roasting for 30–45 minutes.

Any leftover chicken can be used in sandwiches or packed lunches. It would also be perfect in the Chicken and Ham Pie (see page 89) and Quick Chicken Casserole (see page 86).

Keep the carcass for making into stock (see page 20) for future recipes.

SPICY SPATCHCOCK CHICKEN WITH WATERCRESS AND ORANGE SALAD

⊛ ⊖ ⬓

Marinating meat in yoghurt is a fantastic way of adding flavour while keeping it moist. The slight acidity of the yoghurt coating lightly tenderises the meat and ensures no moisture escapes during cooking. The salad provides a glorious array of colour and texture, evocative of the North African dishes that inspired this recipe.

Serves 4–6
1 x 1.5–2.25kg (3lb 5oz–5lb) chicken

For the marinade
200g (7oz) thick natural yoghurt
50ml (2fl oz) olive oil
1 tbsp cumin seeds, toasted and finely ground (see tip opposite)
1 tbsp coriander seeds, toasted and finely ground (see tip opposite)
1 tbsp smoked paprika
Salt and freshly ground black pepper

For the salad
2 oranges
3 tbsp olive oil
1 tbsp lemon juice
½ tsp honey
3–4 cooked beetroot, cut into 8 wedges through the root
125g (4½oz) watercress or rocket leaves
100g (3½oz) pine nuts, toasted (see tip opposite)

First prepare the chicken. To remove the backbone, use very sharp scissors to cut through the chicken on both sides of the bone all the way from the top to the bottom. Remove the backbone and open the chicken out like a book, then place the chicken, breast side up, on your worktop and use the palms of your hands to flatten it out.

With a sharp knife, make a few slashes in the legs.

Place all the marinade ingredients in a bowl, season with salt and pepper and whisk together.

Place the chicken in a wide, shallow dish and pour over the marinade, rubbing it into every crevice, including the cuts in the legs. Cover with cling film and chill for at least 2 hours or overnight.

When you are ready to cook the chicken, preheat the oven to 220°C (425°F), Gas mark 7.

Place the marinated chicken in a roasting tin with all the marinade and bake in the oven for 1–1½ hours (the cooking time will vary greatly depending on the size of the chicken) until cooked (see tip on page 82). Cover the chicken, still in the tin, with foil and leave to rest somewhere warm – such as in the oven, with the heat switched off – while you make the salad.

Peel and segment each orange. Using a small, sharp knife and working over a bowl to catch the juices, cut off the ends, then carefully cut away the peel and pith in a spiral until you have a peeled orange with flesh and no pith. Carefully cut along the edge of each segment, leaving behind the membrane and freeing a wedge of flesh from the pith. Repeat with all the segments and place in the bowl; squeeze the peel and remaining membrane into the bowl to catch any extra juice, then discard. Instead of segmenting the oranges, you could cut each peeled orange into round slices horizontally.

In a small bowl, mix the juice from the oranges with the olive oil, lemon juice, honey and season to taste. Place the orange segments in a larger bowl with the beetroot and watercress or rocket. Drizzle with some or all of the dressing and scatter over the pine nuts.

Carve the chicken and serve with the salad.

(✳) The salad should be eaten within half an hour of being dressed, but if you want to get ahead, make the salad without adding the leaves (it will be fine for a few hours, out of the fridge), then toss with the leaves just before serving.

Leftover meat will keep, chilled, for a couple of days.

(−+) To serve 2–3 people, marinate 4–6 chicken thighs in half the quantities for the marinade, then bake for about 45 minutes and serve with half quantities of the salad ingredients.

(⌁) Leftovers are perfect for a packed lunch or making into sandwiches.

Keep the carcass to make chicken stock (see page 20).

RACHEL'S TIP To toast the seeds/pine nuts, place in a non-stick pan on a medium–high heat and cook for a minute or so, tossing once or twice, until slightly darker in colour and toasted. (The seeds can be toasted together; the pine nuts should be toasted separately.) Tip the toasted seeds into a mortar and crush with a pestle until fine.

SPANISH CHICKEN

This is a recipe that takes its cue from paella, that classic dish whose aromas waft through markets across Spain. It makes a great one-pot meal, bursting with different flavours – the peppers adding their characteristic sweetness and the whole dish infused with that defining Spanish taste of smoked paprika.

Serves 2–4

25g (1oz) plain flour
1 tsp smoked paprika
½ tsp freshly ground black pepper
½ tsp salt
4 chicken thighs, with the skin on
75ml (3fl oz) olive oil
1 onion, peeled and thinly sliced
2 cloves of garlic, peeled and crushed or finely grated
1 yellow or orange pepper and 1 red pepper, deseeded and cut into 2cm (¾in) chunks
500ml (18fl oz) chicken stock mixed with 2 tbsp tomato purée (see tip below)
200g (7oz) basmati or paella rice
200g (7oz) large peeled prawns (preferably raw) (optional)
2 tbsp chopped parsley

In a large bowl, mix together the flour, paprika, black pepper and salt. Add the chicken thighs and toss in the mixture until well coated.

Place a large saucepan or casserole dish on a medium-high heat and pour in 50ml (2fl oz) of the olive oil. Add the chicken pieces and cook for 3–4 minutes on each side or until crisp and deep golden brown. Remove from the pot and set aside.

Pour the remaining oil into the same pan or dish and add the onion and garlic. Sauté, stirring occasionally, for 5 minutes or until almost softened and a little golden around the edges, then add the peppers and cook for a further 5 minutes.

Add the mixed stock and tomato purée and the rice, stirring to mix. Return the chicken to the pot, cover with a lid and simmer gently for 20 minutes or until the chicken is completely cooked (the flesh white all the way through). If using prawns, add them just before the end of cooking time – 5 minutes for raw prawns or 2 minutes for cooked prawns. Scatter with the chopped parsley and serve with a slice of lemon if you like.

(✳) Apart from prepping the vegetables, which can be done a few hours in advance, this is a dish that should be made in one go. It will keep in the fridge for up to two days, however, and can be reheated gently.

(⊖⊕) Halving or doubling the quantities in this recipe would be quite straightforward.

RACHEL'S TIP If using paella rice, you will need an extra 50ml (2fl oz) of stock, approximately. The finished dish should not be dry; it should be quite wet, in fact. If it has cooked a bit too quickly or if it hasn't been covered completely, you will need to add extra stock or water.

HONEY-ROASTED DUCK WITH RED CABBAGE

Crisp and crunchy duck skin must be one of the very best things to eat. Despite the gloriously juicy meat, the skin is still my favourite part of a roast duck. The honey and thyme glaze adds both colour and of course sweetness, while the sweet-sour red cabbage makes an ideal accompanying dish, although roast potatoes and a green vegetable such as kale, or the Cheesy Kale Bake (see page 207), would also go well.

Serves 4–6
1 whole duck (about 1.8kg/4lb)
3 sprigs of thyme and 1 tbsp chopped thyme
Sea salt and freshly ground black pepper
2 tbsp honey
15g (½oz) plain flour
15g (½oz) butter
250ml (9fl oz) chicken or duck stock (see pages 20 and 21)

For the red cabbage
450g (1lb) red cabbage
1 tbsp white wine or cider vinegar
50g (2oz) sugar
450g (1lb) cooking apples

Preheat the oven to 180°C (350°F), Gas mark 4.

Place the duck, breast side up, in a roasting tin. Insert the sprigs of thyme into the cavity of the duck and season with salt and pepper. Sprinkle salt over the skin of the duck, then roast in the oven for 45 minutes.

Meanwhile, mix the honey and chopped thyme together in a small bowl. After the duck has been roasting for 45 minutes, remove from the oven and spread the honey mixture over the skin. Return to the oven and cook for about another 45 minutes or until the duck is cooked to your liking (see tip opposite).

While the duck is cooking, prepare the red cabbage. Remove any damaged outer leaves, then cut the cabbage into quarters, cut away the core and slice the leaves finely across the grain. Put the vinegar into a casserole dish or stainless-steel saucepan with the sugar and add 120ml (4fl oz) of water and 1 level teaspoon of salt. Tip in the cabbage and bring to the boil.

Meanwhile, peel and core the apples and cut into quarters (don't be tempted to cut them smaller). Lay these on top of the cabbage and bring back up to the boil, then reduce the heat to low, cover with a lid and cook gently for 30–50 minutes or until the cabbage is tender. Do not overcook or the colour and flavour will be ruined. Taste for seasoning, adding more sugar if necessary, and keep warm in the pan until the duck is ready.

When the duck is cooked, remove from the roasting tin, cover with foil and place somewhere warm (such as in the oven with the heat switched off) to rest for at least 15 minutes while you make the gravy.

Place the flour and butter in a saucepan on a medium heat. Cook, stirring frequently, for about 2 minutes to make a roux, then set aside.

Place the roasting tin on a medium heat and deglaze with a little of the stock, stirring with a wooden spoon and scraping any sticky bits from the bottom of the tin. Drain off the fat using a separating jug or, if you don't have one, pour the liquid into a bowl and add a handful of ice cubes. After a few minutes the fat will float to the surface. Remove and discard the fat, then pour the remaining liquid into a saucepan with the remaining chicken or duck stock and place on a medium heat.

Bring the stock to the boil, whisk in the roux a little at a time and continue to boil for 2–3 minutes to thicken very slightly. Season to taste with salt and pepper. Just before serving the duck, strain the gravy through a fine sieve into a gravy boat or jug and tip the cooked red cabbage into a warmed serving dish. Carve the duck and serve immediately.

✳ Once cooked, the duck can be kept, covered, in the fridge for up to two days.

Red cabbage can be cooked two days in advance and kept in the fridge. It also freezes very well.

▭ Any leftover meat is ideal for using in the Chinese-style Duck Soup (see page 108) or Duck Plum Spring Rolls (see page 111).

Keep the duck carcass for making into stock (see page 21) for future recipes.

RACHEL'S TIP I like to cook the duck right through so that the legs feel slightly loose when you pull them.

CHINESE-STYLE DUCK SOUP

If you've had a roast duck (see page 104) and find yourself left with the carcass, then I wholeheartedly recommend making this soup. You'll need to make it into stock first, of course (see page 21), but the deep, strong flavour it imparts to the soup is so fabulous that the extra effort is really worth it. It will be a different kind of soup if made with chicken stock, lighter-tasting but still delicious. Whichever stock you go for, homemade is best: the better the stock, the better this soup will be.

Serves 4

100g (3½oz) thin rice noodles
600ml (1 pint) duck or chicken stock (see pages 20 and 21)
2 x 5mm (¼in) slices of root ginger, slightly crushed
150g (5oz) pak choi (or leftover Sesame Pak Choi – see page 198), shredded
2 cloves of garlic, peeled and slightly crushed
150g (5oz) cooked duck (see page 104), finely sliced or shredded
Splash of soy sauce or 1–2 tbsp hoisin sauce

To serve

4 spring onions, trimmed and finely sliced at an angle
2 tbsp roughly chopped coriander

Place the noodles in a bowl, cover with boiling water and leave to stand for the length of time specified in the packet instructions or until softened. Drain in a colander, retaining 50ml (2fl oz) of the soaking liquid, then tip the noodles back in the pan with the reserved liquid and set aside.

Pour the stock into a large saucepan, add the ginger and garlic and bring to the boil. Add the pak choi (if using the raw vegetable) and cook for 1 minute, then tip in the duck (and leftover Sesame Pak Choi, if using) and cook for another minute or until the pak choi is almost tender and the duck heated through. Season with the soy or hoisin sauce.

To serve, divide the cooked noodles between warmed deep soup bowls. Ladle over the soup, first removing the ginger and garlic, then scatter the sliced spring onions and coriander over each bowl.

(✳) This is such a great last-minute recipe that there's no need to prepare anything in advance, though the noodles can be soaked an hour or two before making the soup.

DUCK PLUM SPRING ROLLS

Preparing spring rolls from scratch is absolutely worth the effort. They're not difficult to make, especially if you use leftover duck meat and plum sauce. You could use bought plum sauce here, too, if necessary. A spring roll is at its best just after cooking when the filling is still warm and the outside is hot, crisp and crunchy. Spring roll pastry is available at Asian food shops and some supermarkets.

Makes 8

150g (5oz) cooked duck meat
(see page 104), shredded
50g (2oz) spring onions, trimmed
and thinly shredded
100g (3½oz) grated carrot
2 tbsp chopped coriander
3 tbsp plum sauce (see page 112),
plus extra to serve
Salt and freshly ground black pepper
8 sheets of spring roll pastry (25cm/10in square)
150ml (5fl oz) sunflower or rapeseed oil

In a bowl, mix together the shredded duck with the spring onions, carrot, coriander and plum sauce, seasoning with salt and pepper to taste.

Lay a sheet of spring roll pastry flat on a board. Add a heaped tablespoon of the duck mixture to the pastry and spread out in a line parallel to the end closest to you, leaving a margin of about 3cm (1¼in) from the edge and a gap of about 5cm (2in) between each end of the mixture and the edge of the pastry on the other sides.

Brush a little water on the bare edges of the pastry, then fold in the sides over the filling. Brush with a little water again, then roll up the pastry away from you, making sure you roll it up tightly. Repeat with the remaining mixture and pastry.

Place a large frying pan on a high heat and pour in the oil. When the oil is hot, add the spring rolls – or as many as will fit in comfortably in a single layer – and fry on all sides for 8–10 minutes or until golden brown. Remove from the pan and place on kitchen paper to drain, then repeat with any remaining spring rolls. Serve with extra plum sauce on the side.

⊛ The spring rolls can be assembled (but not fried) and stored, covered, in the fridge for up to two days before cooking.

⊖ If you want to make 16 small spring rolls, instead of eight larger ones – to serve more people as an hors d'oeuvre, for instance – cut each sheet of pastry in half lengthways and roll in the same way using roughly two heaped teaspoons of filling for each spring roll.

DUCK BREASTS WITH PLUM SAUCE AND VEGETABLE STIR-FRY

✳ 🗀

Duck and certain types of fruit are no strangers to each other. Duck with orange is a match made in heaven, and duck with plum sauce is a classic combination, too, the sweet fruit offsetting the rich meat to perfection. I just love this dish of juicy duck and tangy-sweet plum sauce. Plum sauce keeps well too and is particularly good with other fatty meats, especially pork belly.

Serves 4

4 duck breasts, with the skin on
Salt and freshly ground black pepper
25ml (1fl oz) sunflower or rapeseed oil
4 carrots, peeled and finely sliced on an angle
1 small cabbage or ½ medium cabbage, such as savoy, core removed and leaves finely shredded
Bunch of spring onions, trimmed and finely sliced on an angle
2 cloves of garlic, peeled and crushed or finely grated
1 tsp finely grated ginger
2–4 tbsp soy sauce

For the plum sauce

400g (14oz) plums, destoned and flesh quartered
2 shallots, peeled and sliced
50g (2oz) brown sugar
1 tsp grated root ginger
¼ tsp Chinese five spice
25ml (1fl oz) red wine vinegar
200ml (7fl oz) red wine
2 tbsp soy sauce

First make the plum sauce. Put all the ingredients into a small saucepan and place on a medium heat. Bring to the boil, then reduce the heat to low and simmer for 20 minutes or until the plums are very soft. Remove from the heat and whiz in a blender or food processor until smooth. Taste the sauce, seasoning with more soy sauce if necessary.

Next score the duck breasts. Use a sharp knife to cut a grid pattern in the skin and fat, taking care not to cut through the meat. Season and place in a frying pan, skin side down. Set the pan on a low–medium heat and cook the duck for about 10 minutes or until the skin is golden brown and the fat has rendered (see 🗀 below). Flip the duck over and cook for a further 2–3 minutes. Leave to rest somewhere warm for 5 minutes in the pan, then cut into slices (at an angle, if you wish).

While the duck is cooking, stir-fry the vegetables. Place a wok or large frying pan on a high heat and leave for about 5 minutes or until smoking hot. Pour in the oil and add the carrots, stir-frying these for 2 minutes, then add the cabbage, spring onions, garlic, ginger and 2 tablespoons of the soy sauce and cook for just a couple of minutes or until the vegetables are starting to soften but still have a bite. Tip into a serving dish, adding more soy sauce to taste if necessary, and serve with the sliced duck and plum sauce.

✳ The duck and the stir-fried vegetables should be served as soon as they're cooked, but the vegetables can be prepared an hour or so ahead of time.

The plum sauce can be made in advance and stored in the fridge, where it will keep for up to a week; simply reheat to serve. It's also great with the Duck Plum Spring Rolls (see page 111) and Slow-roast Pork Belly (see page 160).

🗀 As the duck fat renders in the frying pan, pour it out into a bowl or jar, reserving it for roasting potatoes another day. It'll keep, covered, in the fridge for about a year!

EGGS & CHEESE

SPINACH, BACON AND GRUYÈRE FRITTATA

A frittata is a most accommodating host, happy to provide a home for to all sorts of leftovers, from cooked potatoes and other vegetables to roast pork or chicken and every kind of grated cheese. This recipe uses fresh ingredients to enable you to create frittata from scratch, but do incorporate whatever leftovers you have to hand.

Serves 4–6
40g (1½oz) butter
350g (12oz) spinach leaves (stalks discarded), washed and shredded
Salt and freshly ground black pepper
1 tbsp olive oil
200g (7oz) rashers of rindless streaky bacon, cut into roughly 2cm (¾in) chunks
8 eggs
175ml (6fl oz) single or regular cream
100g (3½oz) Gruyère cheese, grated

Equipment
25cm (10in) diameter ovenproof frying pan

Preheat the oven to 200°C (400°F), Gas mark 6.

Place the frying pan on a medium heat, add 15g (½oz) of the butter and the spinach leaves, season with salt and pepper and stir over the heat until the spinach wilts. Drain the spinach (see ⬚ below) and set aside.

Place the frying pan back on the heat and add the olive oil. When the oil is hot, add the bacon pieces and cook for 5–10 minutes or until lightly browned. Using a slotted spoon, transfer the bacon pieces (keeping any fat in the pan) to the spinach.

In a large bowl, whisk the eggs with the cream and grated cheese. Mix in the spinach and bacon and season with salt and pepper to taste.

Put the pan back on the heat and add the remaining butter. When the butter is foaming, pour in the egg and cheese mixture and turn the heat down to low. Cook for 3–4 minutes or until the frittata is a light golden colour underneath, then place in the oven and cook for 8–10 minutes or until golden on top and just set in the centre. Slide onto a warmed plate and cut into slices to serve. It can be served hot or at room temperature.

⊘ **Spinach, potato and Gruyère frittata:**
Replace the bacon with the same weight of cooked potatoes, diced to about the same size as the bacon.
Spinach, red pepper and Gruyère frittata:
Replace the bacon with the same weight of raw red pepper, diced to about the same size and then fried like the bacon.

✳ This is so fast to make so there's not much need to prepare ahead, though the spinach could be cooked a couple of hours in advance.

The frittata can be kept somewhere cool for up to 24 hours. To eat warm, place in the oven (preheated to 180°C/350°F/Gas mark 4) to reheat for 10–15 minutes.

⬚ Reserve the spinach cooking liquid to use as a vegetable stock for soup, if you like. Leftovers frittata is perfect for a packed lunch or picnic.

CHEESY BREAD GRATIN

A cross between a savoury bread and butter pudding and a cheese soufflé, this is
perfect for a hearty brunch or late-night supper. It's also a great standby dish that's
ideal for using up leftover scraps of cheese (any mixture of hard cheese would do)
and bread that's no longer fresh. Slightly stale bread is actually best for this recipe,
as it will absorb the egg mixture without disintegrating.

Serves 6–8
2 tbsp olive oil
250g (9oz) rindless streaky bacon (either in
   rashers or in one piece), cut into 0.5 x 2cm
   (¼ x ¾in) pieces
1 slightly stale baguette or loaf, cut into
   roughly 2cm (¾in) slices
200g (7oz) Parmesan cheese, grated
200g (7oz) mozzarella, grated
100g (3½oz) Gruyère cheese, grated
6 eggs
Salt and freshly ground black pepper
100g (3½oz) Cheddar cheese, grated
2 tbsp chopped chives

Equipment
20 x 30cm (8 x 12in) ovenproof dish

Preheat the oven to 220°C (425°F), Gas mark 7.

Place a large frying pan on a high heat and
add the olive oil. When the oil is hot, tip in the
bacon pieces and cook for 5–10 minutes or until
browned and slightly crisp.

While the bacon is cooking, lay out the bread
slices in the ovenproof dish. When the bacon is
cooked, remove from the pan with a slotted spoon
and scatter over the bread.

Place the Parmesan, mozzarella and Gruyère
in a food processor with the eggs and whiz for
about 1 minute or until smooth. Season with salt
and pepper to taste.

Pour the egg and cheese mixture over the
bread and bacon, then sprinkle over the grated
Cheddar and chopped chives and season with
pepper. Place the dish in the oven and bake for
15–20 minutes or until just set in the middle and
puffed up and golden brown on top. Serve with
a green salad.

⊘ For a vegetarian version of this dish, simply
omit the bacon.

✳ This dish can be prepared an hour or two in
advance, then cooked when you're ready to eat.
It can also be frozen before it's baked – it will
keep, covered, in the freezer for up to three
months. Defrost completely before cooking.

⊕ The quantities in this recipe can be halved or
multiplied depending on the number of people
you're serving.

CHEESE, TOMATO AND BASIL TART

Sweet ripe tomatoes and aromatic basil provide the perfect foil for the intense savouriness of the cheese in this dish. The tart is equally delicious served warm, straight from the oven, or cold for a picnic or packed lunch.

Serves 4–6
1 shortcrust pastry tart case, cooked 'blind'
   (see page 54)

For the filling
10 ripe tomatoes, halved widthways
2 tbsp olive oil
½ tsp sugar
Salt and freshly ground black pepper
25g (1oz) butter
1 onion, peeled and finely chopped
2 eggs
200ml (7fl oz) double or regular cream
2 tbsp torn or sliced basil
150g (5oz) Cheddar cheese, grated

Preheat the oven to 180°C (350°F), Gas mark 4.

Place the tomatoes on a baking tray, drizzle with the olive oil and sprinkle with the sugar and ½ teaspoon of salt. Place in the oven and bake for about 45 minutes or until completely softened and a little browned around the edges. Remove from the oven and allow to cool.

Meanwhile, place a frying pan on a medium heat and add the butter. When melted and foaming, add the onion and cook, stirring occasionally, for about 10 minutes or until golden. Remove from the heat and set aside to cool.

In a bowl, whisk together the eggs and cream, stir in the basil, and season with salt and pepper.

Spread out the fried onion pieces in a layer in the blind-baked tart case. Top with two-thirds of the cheese, then arrange the cooked tomato halves on top. Next pour in the egg mixture and top with the remaining cheese. Place in the oven and bake for 30–40 minutes or until golden brown on top and just set in the centre.

✳ The cooked tart can be kept somewhere cool, preferably not in fridge, for up to 24 hours and reheated at in a moderate oven (preheated to 180°C/350°F/Gas mark 4) for 10–15 minutes.

⌂ Leftovers are perfect for a packed lunch or picnic.

FRIED EGGS WITH CHORIZO, ONIONS AND POTATOES

For me this is a true storecupboard supper. I know not everyone will have chorizo immediately to hand, but it's quite easy to get hold of and I adore it so much my fridge is rarely without it. The strong paprika flavour can be used to enhance all sorts of dishes and it goes especially well with eggs. You could also serve this dish as a Spanish-style brunch.

Serves 4

750g (1lb 10oz) potatoes, or leftover cooked potatoes, peeled and cut into roughly 2cm (¾in) chunks
Salt and freshly ground black pepper
2 tbsp olive oil
275g (10oz) onions, peeled and sliced
200g (7oz) chorizo, cut into 5mm (¼in) slices
1 tsp smoked paprika
2 tbsp chopped parsley
25g (1oz) butter
4 eggs

If using raw potatoes, fill a large saucepan with water, add a good pinch of salt and place on a high heat. Bring to the boil, then add the potatoes and boil for 6–10 minutes or just until tender.

Place a large frying pan on a high heat and add half the olive oil. When the oil is hot, add the onions and season with salt and pepper, then sauté for about 8 minutes or until almost softened and a little golden around the edges.

When the potatoes are cooked, drain in a colander, then tip them into the onions and continue to sauté for another 6–8 minutes or until the onions are golden.

Add the chorizo and paprika and cook for 4–5 minutes, tossing regularly. Season to taste with salt and pepper and add the chopped parsley. Tip into a warmed dish and set aside while you fry the eggs.

Clean the pan, then place back on a high heat and add the butter and remaining oil. When the butter is foaming, crack in the eggs to fry them, tilting the pan and spooning the melted butter and oil over the eggs as they cook. When they are cooked to your liking, place the eggs on top of the chorizo, onions and potatoes in the dish. Alternatively, divide the chorizo mixture between individual plates and serve each with a fried egg on top.

✳ The potato and chorizo mixture can be cooked an hour or two in advance, then reheated on a high heat in the frying pan. The eggs, once they are fried, need to be served straight away.

⊶ The quantities can be halved or multiplied, depending on how many you're feeding.

CRUNCHY MACARONI AND CHEESE

Macaroni and cheese is such a soothing and comforting dish. A crowd-pleaser that rarely needs embellishment, it can be a fantastic vehicle for leftover cooked ham (see page 171) even so, the meat providing juicy nuggets of extra flavour. I also like to add a little crunch to offset the smooth pasta and sauce. Here breadcrumbs are mixed with melted butter to form a divinely crisp crust when the dish is baked in the oven.

Serves 4
200g (7oz) macaroni or other pasta, such as
   conchiglie, farfalle or penne
Salt and freshly ground black pepper
400g (14oz) cooked ham (see page 171),
   cut into 0.5 x 1–2cm (¼ x ½–¾in) strips
135g (5oz) butter
35g (1¼oz) plain flour
500ml (18fl oz) milk
300g (11oz) Cheddar or Gruyère cheese, grated
2 tsp Dijon mustard
200g (7oz) breadcrumbs

Equipment
20 x 30cm (8 x 12in) ovenproof dish

Preheat the oven to 200°C (400°F), Gas mark 6.

First cook the macaroni. Bring a large saucepan of water to the boil, add the pasta and stir in 1 teaspoon of salt, then cook for the length of time specified in the packet instructions or until al dente. Drain in a colander, retaining about 50ml (2fl oz) of the cooking water, then tip the pasta into the ovenproof dish with the reserved liquid. (The liquid will be absorbed by the pasta as it sits, preventing it from sticking together.) Scatter the pieces of cooked ham over the pasta and set aside while you make the cheese sauce.

Melt 35g (1¼oz) of the butter in a clean saucepan on a medium heat, then whisk in the flour and cook, stirring frequently, for 1 minute. Pour in the milk and bring to the boil, whisking continuously, then take off the heat and stir in the cheese and mustard. Season to taste with salt and pepper, and a little more mustard if needed, then pour the sauce over the pasta and ham.

Melt the remaining butter in a separate pan. Remove from the heat and mix in the breadcrumbs, then sprinkle over the sauce. Place the dish in the oven and bake for about 30 minutes or until the breadcrumbs are golden and the sauce is bubbling. Serve with a green salad, if you wish.

⊘ Simply leave out the ham for a vegetarian version of this dish.

✳ This dish can be prepared in advance up to the point of assembling everything in the dish. Keep covered in the fridge for 48 hours or in the freezer for up to three months. (If frozen, it will need to defrost completely before cooking.) Bake in the oven as above.

Once cooked, it will keep in the fridge for up to three days; reheat in the oven (preheated to 180°C/350°F/Gas mark 4) for about 30 minutes before serving.

⊝ If using an ovenproof dish with half the volume of the one recommended here, you can halve the quantities in this recipe quite easily. The cooking time will be a little less – just make sure the crumbs are golden and the sauce is bubbling. You could also multiply the quantities if you're feeding a crowd.

BEEF & LAMB

CHEESY MEATBALLS WITH SPAGHETTI

I love this comforting and homely dish – a firm favourite with the family, as I suspect it will be with yours too. Meatballs in tomato sauce is a classic dish, which I've tweaked a little here by baking them with a bit of Gruyère sprinkled on top. I've used spaghetti but any other long type of pasta would work equally well.

Serves 4–5
100g (3½oz) Gruyère cheese, grated
400g (14oz) spaghetti or other pasta, such
   as fettuccine, linguine or tagliatelle
15g (½oz) butter

For the meatballs
500g (1lb 2oz) minced beef or pork, or 250g
   (9oz) minced beef and 250g (9oz) minced pork
1 small onion, peeled and grated or very
   finely chopped
2 cloves of garlic, crushed or finely grated
1 tsp chopped thyme leaves
Salt and freshly ground black pepper
Olive oil, for frying

For the tomato sauce
1 x 400g tin of chopped tomatoes, or 400g
   (14oz) ripe tomatoes, peeled (see tip below)
   and chopped
1 tbsp sugar
1 tbsp tomato paste
2 sprigs of thyme

Equipment
23cm (9in) diameter ovenproof dish

First, make the meatballs. In a bowl, mix together the minced meat with the onion, garlic and thyme and season with salt and pepper. Set a large frying pan on a high heat, add a small drizzle of olive oil and allow it to get hot. Place a small amount of the meat mixture, about a teaspoonful, in the pan and cook. Then taste it for seasoning, adding more salt, pepper or thyme to the meat mixture in the bowl if you think it needs it. When you're happy with the flavour, roll the mixture into 24 balls.

Pour 3 tablespoons of olive oil into the frying pan and place back on a high heat. When the oil is hot, add the meatballs or as many as will fit in easily with a bit of space in between. Cook, stirring or tossing frequently, for about 5 minutes or until well browned all over, then transfer to the ovenproof dish and set aside. Repeat with the remaining meatballs, if you're cooking them in batches, adding more oil to the pan if necessary.

Meanwhile, preheat the oven to 180°C (350°F), Gas mark 4.

As the meatballs cook, place all the sauce ingredients in a saucepan. Season with salt and pepper, then simmer, uncovered, for 15 minutes or until the tomatoes have softened and the sauce has thickened slightly. Pour the tomato sauce over the meatballs in the ovenproof dish and scatter over the grated cheese. Place the dish in the oven and cook for 15–20 minutes or until the sauce is bubbling and the cheese melted and golden.

While the meatballs are in the oven, cook the spaghetti in a large saucepan of water on a high heat, with 1 teaspoon of salt, according to the

RACHEL'S TIP To peel the tomatoes, use a sharp knife to score a cross in the base of each one, cutting through the skin. Place the tomatoes in a bowl and cover with boiling water, leaving them in the water for 15–20 seconds. Drain and rinse in cold water, then peel away the skin – it should come away very easily.

packet instructions or until al dente. Drain in a colander, retaining about 50ml (2fl oz) of the cooking liquid, then tip the pasta back into the pan with the reserved liquid and stir in the butter. Serve with the meatballs in tomato sauce.

✳ The raw meatballs will keep, covered, in the fridge for two days and in the freezer for up to three months. These are the same meatballs as in the Meatball Skewers (see page 137). I usually make twice the amount and freeze half the batch for another day.

This dish is best eaten on the same day it's made, although it can be kept in the fridge overnight and reheated the following day.

The tomato sauce will keep happily in the fridge for up to four days and in the freezer for up to three months. Reheat on the hob and mix with freshly cooked pasta for a quick and simple dish.

⊖⊕ The quantities in this recipe would be fine halved or doubled. If doubling, though, you will still need to cook the meatballs in batches in the frying pan so as not to crowd them and ensuring they brown properly. You will need either two dishes or one larger one, bearing in mind that the latter will take longer to cook.

TAGLIATELLE AL RAGÙ

'Ragù' in Italian describes a meat-based sauce specifically for mixing with pasta, and it comes in many guises. The one I've used here is based on the classic *ragù alla bolognese*, and would of course go with spaghetti as well as other kinds of long pasta. I have recently started using minced pork in the recipe, too, as I love the slightly sweet flavour that it brings. But whether it's all beef, all pork or half of each, the key to a great ragù is long, slow cooking.

Serves 6–8

500g (1lb 2oz) tagliatelle or other pasta, such as linguine, pappardelle or spaghetti
50g (2oz) Parmesan cheese, grated, to serve

For the ragù

3 tbsp olive oil
1 large onion (about 250g/9oz), peeled and finely diced
3 cloves of garlic, peeled and crushed or finely grated
3 sticks of celery, trimmed and finely diced
1 leek, trimmed and finely diced
Salt and freshly ground black pepper
1kg (2lb 3oz) minced beef or pork, or 500g (1lb 2oz) minced beef and 500g (1lb 2oz) minced pork
1 bay leaf
2 x 400g tins of chopped tomatoes, or 800g (1¾lb) ripe tomatoes, peeled (see tip on page 128) and chopped
2 tbsp tomato purée
200ml (7fl oz) white or red wine
2–3 tbsp sugar

Preheat the oven (if not cooking the ragù on the hob) to 150°C (300°F), Gas mark 2.

First make the ragù. Place a large casserole dish or saucepan (ovenproof, if necessary) on a medium heat and add the olive oil. When the oil is hot, tip in the onion, garlic, celery and leek. Season with salt and pepper and cook, uncovered, for 8–10 minutes, stirring every so often, until the vegetables have softened. Turn the heat up to high, add the meat and stir to break up the mince, cooking until no traces of pink remain.

Add the bay leaf with the chopped tomatoes, tomato purée, wine and sugar, and bring to the boil. If using the oven, cover the dish or pan with a lid and cook for about 1 hour. If cooking on the hob, reduce the heat to low and simmer for about 1 hour, uncovered and stirring regularly. When cooked, the sauce will have thickened and the tomatoes softened completely. Taste for seasoning, adding more salt and pepper if necessary.

Shortly before the sauce has finished cooking, prepare the tagliatelle. Place a large saucepan of salted water on a high heat and bring to the boil. Add the pasta and cook for the length of time specified in the packet instructions or until just al dente. Drain in a colander, retaining about 50ml (2fl oz) of the cooking liquid, then tip the pasta back into the pan with the reserved liquid.

Add the sauce to the pasta and stir together. (Add as much sauce as you think you'll need – you can always save the rest for another day.) Divide between individual plates, sprinkling over the grated Parmesan to serve.

✱ The ragù is also used in the Classic Lasagne (see page 133). I like to make double quantities and then freeze half to use with lasagne or pasta. The cooked sauce can be frozen for up to three months and will otherwise keep in the fridge for up to three days.

CLASSIC LASAGNE

A firm favourite in our house, lasagne is great for feeding a hungry crowd. With a bit of forward planning, you can save time preparing the dish by using ragù that you've already made (see page 130).

Serves 6–8

1 quantity of cooked ragù (see page 130)
12–16 sheets of fresh or precooked dried lasagne (see tip below)
100g (3½oz) Cheddar cheese, grated
50g (2oz) Parmesan cheese, grated

For the cheese sauce

70g (2½oz) butter
70g (2½oz) plain flour
1 litre (1¾ pints) milk
200g (7oz) Cheddar cheese, grated
1 tsp Dijon mustard

Equipment

20 x 30cm (8 x 12in) ovenproof dish

Preheat the oven to 180°C (350°F), Gas mark 4.

First make the cheese sauce. Melt the butter in a saucepan on a medium heat, then whisk in the flour and cook, stirring frequently, for 1 minute. Gradually pour in the milk and bring to the boil, whisking continuously until the sauce has thickened. Remove from the heat and whisk in the cheese and mustard, seasoning with salt and pepper to taste, then set aside.

Place a thin layer of ragù in the bottom of the ovenproof dish, cover with a layer of the cheese sauce, then add lasagne sheets to cover the sauce, in a single layer. Repeat this process, finishing with a layer of pasta topped with cheese sauce only.

Sprinkle over both cheeses, then bake in the oven for 45–50 minutes or until golden brown and bubbling hot. Serve with a green salad if you wish.

⊛ The lasagne can be prepared in advance up to the stage before baking and either stored in the freezer (if the ragù hasn't already been frozen), well covered, for up to three months or in the fridge for 48 hours. If frozen, it'll need to be defrosted before being baked as above.

Once cooked, the lasagne will keep in the fridge for up to three days; it can also be frozen for up to three months. It is best eaten after reheating properly in the oven (preheated to 180°C/350°F/Gas mark 4) for about 40 minutes. Cover in foil for the first 30–35 minutes, then remove for the last few minutes to crisp the top.

⊖ If you've a dish with half the volume, you can halve the quantities in this recipe quite easily. The cooking time will be a little less – just make sure it's golden brown and bubbling hot. You could also double the quantities and make it in either two dishes or one larger one, bearing in mind that the latter will take longer to cook.

RACHEL'S TIP Depending on the depth of the dish, and allowing four sheets of lasagne per layer, 12 sheets should give you three layers of pasta and 16 sheets four layers.

ENCHILADAS

This recipe is much like a Mexican-style pasta bake, where the whole point of the dish is that the cheese is cooked in the oven where it melts and browns into a gorgeous topping. Enchiladas can take all manner of different fillings; I've filled the ones here with a rich beef and pepper mixture that goes especially well with the melted cheese and lime chive cream.

Serves 4

2 tbsp olive oil

500g (1lb 2oz) minced beef

300g (11oz) ripe tomatoes, cut into 1cm (½in) chunks, or 300g (11oz) cherry tomatoes, halved

300ml (½ pint) tomato passata (see tip below)

2 tsp sugar

2 generous tbsp chopped coriander

8 x 20cm (8in) diameter wheat-flour tortillas

200g (7oz) Cheddar cheese, or a mixture of Cheddar and mozzarella, grated

For the roasted vegetables

1 red pepper, deseeded and cut into 1cm (½in) chunks

1 yellow pepper, deseeded and cut into 1cm (½in) chunks

1 red onion, peeled and cut into 1cm (½in) chunks

3 cloves of garlic, peeled and finely chopped

1 fresh red chilli pepper, deseeded (optional) and finely chopped

2 tbsp olive oil

Salt and freshly ground black pepper

2 spring onions, trimmed and cut at an angle into 1cm (½in) slices

For the lime chive cream

200g (7oz) sour cream

1 tsp finely chopped chives

Squeeze of lime juice

Preheat oven to 220°C (425°F), Gas mark 7.

First roast the vegetables. In a bowl, toss together the red and yellow peppers, onion, garlic and chilli pepper with the olive oil and season with salt and pepper. Tip into a roasting tin and place in the oven to cook for 10 minutes, then remove from the oven and stir in the spring onions. Return to the oven to roast for a further 5–10 minutes or until all the vegetables are tender. Take out of the oven but leave it switched on for cooking the filled enchiladas.

While the vegetables are roasting, place a large frying pan on a high heat and add the 2 tablespoons of olive oil. When the oil is hot, add the minced beef and cook, stirring frequently, for about 5 minutes or until well browned. Add the tomatoes, passata and sugar, then bring to a simmer and cook, uncovered, for about 10 minutes or until the tomatoes are tender and the sauce has thickened.

Meanwhile, prepare the lime chive cream. Mix together all the ingredients in a small bowl, season with salt and pepper and set aside. Brush a baking tray or roasting tin with olive oil.

When the meat sauce is cooked, stir in the roasted vegetables and the chopped coriander, then remove from the heat and season with salt and pepper to taste. Either set aside to cool down or use straight away while it's still hot.

To assemble the enchiladas, lay the tortillas out on your work surface and divide the meat and vegetable mixture between them, spooning

RACHEL'S TIP If you don't have any passata, just whiz up half a 400g tin of tomatoes with 100ml (3½ fl oz) of water.

it down the centre of each tortilla while leaving a gap of 3–4cm (1¼–1½in) at the top and bottom edges. Fold over the bottom edge of each tortilla to overlap the mixture by 3–4cm (1¼–1½in), then fold over both sides of the tortilla to overlap in the centre.

Arrange the filled enchiladas side by side on the prepared baking tray or roasting tin, then scatter with the grated cheese. Place in the oven for 10–20 minutes or until the cheese is melted and golden brown and the filling piping hot. Serve the enchiladas with the lime chive cream. Guacamole and Tomato Salsa (see page 74) are also great with these.

(✳) The enchiladas can be made ahead right up to the stage before baking. They will keep, covered, for up to 24 hours in the fridge. Once cooked, they are definitely best eaten straight away.

(⊖) The quantities can be halved, but using the same amount of olive oil for cooking the vegetables and meat. You can also double the quantities, but you'll need to use two baking trays/roasting tins for cooking the filled enchiladas.

MEATBALL SKEWERS

What I love about this dish is that you can make the meatballs ahead of time; you could even make up the skewers in advance so that cooking is simply a matter of baking in the oven. This would be delicious served with the Pickled Beetroot, Sweet Potato and Lentil Salad (see page 193).

Makes 8 skewers
3 red onions, peeled and each cut into 8 wedges
50ml (2fl oz) olive oil, plus extra for drizzling

For the meatballs
500g (1lb 2oz) minced beef or pork, or 250g
   (9oz) minced beef and 250g (9oz) minced pork
1 small onion, peeled and grated or very
   finely chopped
2 cloves of garlic, crushed or finely grated
1 tsp chopped thyme leaves
Salt and freshly ground black pepper

Equipment
8 metal or wooden skewers

Preheat the oven to 220°C (425°F), Gas mark 7, or heat up the grill or barbecue. If using wooden skewers, soak in cold water for 30 minutes to prevent them from burning during cooking.

To make the meatballs, mix together the minced meat with the onion, garlic and thyme and season with salt and pepper. Set a large frying pan on a high heat, add a small drizzle of olive oil and allow it to get hot. Place a small amount of the meat mixture, about a teaspoonful, in the pan and cook. Then taste it for seasoning, adding more salt, pepper or thyme to the meat mixture in the

bowl if you think it needs it. When you're happy with the flavour, roll the mixture into 24 balls.

Divide the meatballs between the skewers, alternating them with the onion wedges, then place on a baking sheet and drizzle with the olive oil. Bake in the oven for 10–12 minutes or until the meatballs are cooked and the onion wedges tender and light golden.

⊘ Feel free to add other vegetables to these skewers, such as chunks of red or yellow pepper, courgette or aubergine.

✳ The raw meatballs will keep, covered, in the fridge for two days and in the freezer for up to three months. These are the same meatballs as in the Cheesy Meatballs with Spaghetti (see page 128). I usually make twice the amount and freeze half the batch for another day.

Once cooked, these skewers are best served right away, or stored for up to 24 hours in the fridge.

⊝ You could easily halve or double the quantities in this recipe.

▢ Eat leftover meatballs either cold or reheated, with a little sauce such as mayonnaise or tomato sauce (see page 128).

STEAK FAJITAS

This is one of my family's favourite feasts. It involves a little work, but all the different elements come together in an unparalleled celebration of flavour. "Faja" means "belt" or "strip" in Spanish, so "fajita" means "little strip", which explains the long, thin pieces of beef in this great Tex-Mex meal. Beef skirt of flank is the traditional cut used, but other beef cuts, chicken, pork or seafood can be used instead. Here, the steak, juicy and tender from being marinated in the spices and lime juice, is complemented by the soft beans, tasty enough on their own to replace the meat for a vegetarian version of this dish. The Tomato Salsa and Guacamole (see recipes on page 74) add a fresh and spicy touch, offset by the cooling sour cream and wonderfully savoury cheese. Set aside a little time to make this meal – much of it can be made ahead and I promise it will be worth it!

Makes 8 fajitas
1–2 flank or skirt steaks (about 400g/14oz in total)
1–2 tbsp olive oil
8 x 20cm (8in) diameter wheat-flour tortillas

For the marinade
Juice of 1 lime
2 tbsp olive oil
2 cloves of garlic, peeled and crushed
 or finely grated
1 tsp freshly ground cumin (see tip opposite)
1 tsp freshly ground coriander (see tip opposite)
1 fresh green chilli pepper, deseeded (optional)
 and finely chopped
Handful of fresh coriander (leaves and small
 stems), chopped

For the refried black beans
50g (2oz) butter
1 large red onion, peeled and finely chopped
2–4 cloves of garlic, peeled and very
 finely chopped
1 fresh red chilli pepper, deseeded (optional)
 and finely chopped
1 tsp freshly ground cumin (see tip opposite)
1 x 400g tin of black or pinto beans, drained
 and rinsed, or 125g (4½oz) dried beans,
 soaked and cooked (see tip opposite)
75ml (3fl oz) vegetable or chicken stock
 (see page 20) or water
Salt and freshly ground black pepper

To serve
1 quantity of Tomato Salsa (see page 74)
1 quantity of Guacamole (see page 74)
250g (9oz) sour cream or crème fraîche
175g (6oz) Cheddar cheese, grated
Lime wedges (optional)

Mix together all the ingredients for the marinade in a shallow bowl, then add the steak and coat in the mixture. Cover and place in the fridge for at least an hour, or up to 3 hours.

Shortly before the steak has finished marinating, prepare the refried black beans. Melt the butter in a wide saucepan or frying pan on a medium heat, then add the onion, garlic, chilli and cumin. Gently fry for 6–8 minutes or until soft and slightly golden around the edges. Tip the cooked beans into the pan and continue to cook the mixture, uncovered, for 3 minutes or until heated through.

Using a potato masher or fork, mash the bean mixture, keeping it chunky and not too smooth. Pour in the stock, then bring to a simmer and cook for 4–5 minutes, uncovered, until the mixture is quite thick. Season to taste with salt and pepper and keep in the pan until you're ready to serve, reheating if necessary.

When the steak has finished marinating, place a griddle pan or a frying pan on a high heat for about 5 minutes to heat up. Add the olive oil to the pan, then add the steak with any marinade coating it. Season with salt and pepper and cook for just a few minutes on each side, depending on how rare you like your meat. When you turn the steak over, season the other side with salt and pepper too. Remove from the heat and allow to rest for 5 minutes before cutting into slices about 5mm (¼in) thick.

Divide the steak slices between the tortillas, adding a spoonful of refried black beans, Tomato Salsa and Guacamole to each, along with a dollop of sour cream and a sprinkling of grated cheese. Fold the bottom edge of each tortilla to overlap the filling by 3–4cm (1¼–1½in) and fold in the sides to overlap in the centre, then place two completed fajitas on each plate to serve.

Alternatively, place the tortillas, steak slices and other accompaniments in separate serving dishes and let people assemble the fajitas themselves, with lime wedges if liked.

⊘ **Refried bean fajitas:** Leave out the steak, and fill the tortillas with the refried black beans, salsa, guacamole, sour cream and cheese.

✳ The refried beans can be made up to two days ahead, stored in the fridge and reheated to serve.

⊕ You can halve or double the quantities in this recipe.

RACHEL'S TIPS   For freshly ground cumin and coriander, use a pestle and mortar to grind the whole seeds, or place in a plastic bag and crush with a rolling pin.

To cook the dried beans, first soak them in plenty of cold water overnight. Drain and place in a saucepan filled with fresh water. Place on a high heat and bring to the boil, then reduce the heat and simmer for ¾–1 hour or until tender. Remove from the heat, drain in a colander and allow to cool.

LAMB KOFTA TAGINE

Please don't be put off by the long list of ingredients here! You'll have most of them in your cupboard already, and even if you have to buy some of the other items, you won't regret it as this wonderfully aromatic dish will be well worth the effort. You can make the kofta up to two days ahead, what's more, which makes cooking on the day very straightforward. Serve hot with buttery couscous, Golden Couscous (see page 191) or flatbreads (see page 27).

Serves 4–6
1 tbsp olive oil
15g (½oz) butter
1 onion, peeled and chopped
2–3 cloves of garlic, peeled and crushed or finely grated
2 tsp finely chopped root ginger
¼–½ fresh red chilli pepper, deseeded (optional) and finely chopped
2 tsp ground turmeric
2 tbsp lemon juice
2 tbsp chopped coriander
1 x 400g tin of chopped tomatoes, or 400g (14oz) ripe tomatoes, peeled (see tip on page 128) and chopped
1 tsp sugar
2 tbsp chopped mint

For the kofta
500g (1lb 2oz) minced lamb or beef
125g (4½oz) very finely chopped or grated onion
2 tbsp chopped parsley
1 tsp ground cinnamon
1 tsp freshly ground cumin
1 tsp freshly ground coriander
¼ tsp cardamom seeds from green cardamom pods (see tip below)
½ tsp paprika
Salt and freshly ground black pepper

Preheat the oven (if not cooking the tagine on the hob) to 150°C (300°F), Gas mark 2.

Place the oil and butter in a large casserole dish or saucepan (ovenproof if necessary) and set over a medium heat. When the butter has melted, add the onion, garlic, ginger and chilli and cook, stirring occasionally, for 6–8 minutes or until they begin to turn lightly golden brown.

Add the turmeric, 1 tablespoon of the lemon juice and half the chopped coriander. Tip in the tomatoes and add the sugar, then bring the mixture to the boil. Reduce the heat and simmer, covered with a lid, for 10 minutes.

Meanwhile make the kofta. Place all the ingredients in a bowl and season with salt and pepper, then mix together thoroughly with your hands. To taste for seasoning, break off a bite-sized piece and fry in a little oil, then add more salt and pepper to the mixture if you think it needs it.

To form the kofta, roll pieces of the mixture and shape them into about 30 little balls each about the size of a walnut in its shell.

Using a spoon, carefully lower the kofta into the tomato mixture and poach, covered, for about 20 minutes, rolling them in the sauce occasionally. Alternatively, cook in the oven for the same length of time. Taste the sauce for seasoning, adding more salt and pepper if needed, then remove from the heat, stir in the remaining lemon juice and sprinkle with the mint and the rest of the coriander.

RACHEL'S TIP Crush the cardamom pods using a pestle and mortar, or the end of a rolling pin, to obtain the seeds.

LAMB NECK WITH YOGHURT, CUCUMBER AND MINT

Like other less-used cuts of meat, neck of lamb is relatively cheap, yet when treated well
– with long, slow cooking – its flavour and texture are unbeatable! You just let your oven
do the work, slowly rendering the fat and breaking down the meat so that it's soft and
meltingly tender. Ask your butcher for the whole neck (you may need to order it in
advance, as it often comes filleted). This dish is particularly good with Golden
Couscous (see page 191), which soaks up all the lamb's juices.

Serves 4

1.25kg (2¾lb) neck of lamb (on the bone)
1 tsp coriander seeds
1 tsp cumin seeds
1 tsp sea salt flakes
½ tsp black peppercorns
15g (½oz) butter, softened
2 cloves of garlic, peeled and crushed
  or finely grated

For the yoghurt with cucumber and mint

250g (9oz) thick natural yoghurt, such as
  Greek yoghurt
¼ cucumber, cut into roughly 1cm (½in) cubes
Juice of ½ lemon
2 tbsp chopped mint
Salt and freshly ground black pepper

Preheat the oven to 140°C (275°F), Gas mark 1.
Using a sharp knife, score the lamb in a grid pattern
(forming roughly 2cm/¾in squares), cutting
through the fat, but taking care not to cut into
the meat.

Place a small saucepan or frying pan on a high
heat and add the coriander and cumin seeds.
Cook the seeds, tossing every now and then, for
1–2 minutes or until they have darkened slightly
in colour. Tip into a mortar with the salt and
peppercorns and crush with a pestle until slightly
coarse, or place in a plastic bag and crush with
a rolling pin instead.

Place the lamb in a roasting tin and rub the
softened butter all over it, then the garlic. Scatter
the spice mix all over the lamb, pressing it in to
help it stick to the butter. Place the spice-coated
lamb in the oven and cook for about 4 hours or
until the meat is meltingly tender and golden
brown on the outside.

Just before the lamb is cooked (though the
cooked lamb will sit somewhere warm for about
an hour), prepare the yoghurt with cucumber
and mint. Place all the ingredients in a bowl
and mix together, seasoning with salt and pepper
to taste.

Carve the lamb into chunks and serve with the
yoghurt and cucumber and Golden Couscous
(see page 191).

✳ The cooked lamb, if you have any left over,
will keep for up to three days in the fridge.

⌂ Any leftover meat could be used in Shepherd's
Pie (see page 154). It would also be delicious on
the Lamb, Feta and Chard Pizza (see page 36) or
in the Lamb and Pearl Barley Broth (see page
153) or Pulled Lamb Toasted Baps (see page 150).

SLOW-ROASTED LAMB WITH BEANS

Long, slow roasting is the best way to cook shoulder of lamb; the fat lubricates the meat, which becomes tenderised and softened. The onions in this dish really benefit from the slow roasting too: cooked in a layer beneath the lamb, where they are soaked in the delicious juices from the meat, they taste utterly divine. Mixed with the beans and some cream, the resulting sauce is quite extraordinary – so good that you almost don't need the lamb!

Serves 8–12
50ml (2fl oz) olive oil
500g (1lb 2oz) onions, peeled and sliced
Salt and freshly ground black pepper
2kg (4lb 4oz) shoulder of lamb, boned, rolled
    and tied (ask your butcher to do this for you)
6 sprigs of thyme and 2 tbsp chopped thyme leaves
4 cloves of garlic, peeled
2 x 400g tins of cannellini beans, drained and
    rinsed, or 250g (9oz) dried cannellini beans,
    soaked and cooked (see tip opposite)
200ml (7fl oz) double or regular cream

Preheat the oven to 110°C (225°F), Gas mark ¼
(see tip, opposite).

Place a casserole dish or saucepan large enough to fit the lamb on a low heat and add 3 tbsp of the olive oil. When the oil is hot, add the onions and season with salt and pepper, then cook very gently, stirring occasionally, for 1 hour or until they are soft, golden and caramelised.

Meanwhile, place a large frying pan on a high heat and add the remaining oil. Season the lamb generously all over with salt and pepper, then cook for about 10 minutes, turning every couple of minutes, until the fat is golden brown.

Place the lamb on top of the cooked onions, then add the sprigs of thyme and the garlic, cover with a lid and place in the oven to cook for about 6 hours or until completely tender.

Take the lamb out of the oven (keeping it switched on) and transfer to a warmed plate, then cover in foil and place back in the oven to keep warm.

Drain the onions, thyme and garlic in a sieve set over a bowl. Leave the liquid to sit for 5 minutes to let the fat rise to the top (add a few ice cubes, if you like, to help speed up the process), then spoon off the fat.

Discarding the sprigs of thyme, transfer the onions and garlic back to the casserole dish or saucepan. Stir in the beans, cream and chopped thyme and simmer for about 5 minutes or until all the flavours have mingled and the beans have absorbed some of the flavour of the sauce. Season to taste with salt and pepper.

Remove the string from the lamb, then carve and serve in slices with the onions and beans.

✳ The lamb can be kept warm in a low oven for up to 1 hour, but then is best eaten straight away. It can otherwise be kept, stored in the fridge, for up to three days.

⊖⊕ The quantities in this recipe can be halved or multiplied, depending on how many people you're serving.

🗇 Any leftover cooked lamb can be made into soup, such as the Lamb and Pearl Barley Broth (see page 153), or used in Shepherd's Pie (see page 154) or for the Lamb, Feta and Chard Pizza (see page 36) or Pulled Lamb Toasted Baps (see page 150).

RACHEL'S TIPS   To cook the dried beans, first soak them in plenty of cold water overnight. Drain and place in a saucepan filled with fresh water. Place on a high heat and bring to the boil, then reduce the heat and simmer for ¾–1 hour or until tender. Remove from the heat, drain in a colander and allow to cool.

For slightly faster-roasted lamb, preheat the oven to 140°C (275°F), Gas mark 1 and cook for about 3 hours. The meat will still be deliciously tender, if not quite as tender as when cooked for longer at a lower temperature.

PULLED LAMB TOASTED BAPS

These big meaty sandwiches are full of the flavours of Greece, from the slow-cooked lamb to the crisp fresh cucumber and intense salty feta – a glorious taste of the Mediterranean. The leftover cooked lamb should ideally be warm or at room temperature (see tip below) to ensure that it's really good and juicy.

Makes 4 baps
4 large white or brown rolls or baps
Butter, for spreading
300g (11oz) shredded cooked lamb
   (see page 146)
¼ cucumber, sliced
½ red onion, peeled and thinly sliced
200g (7oz) feta cheese, sliced
Handful of green leaves, such as rocket
   or watercress

For the lemon aïoli
2–4 cloves of garlic, peeled and crushed
   or finely grated
2 egg yolks
1 tbsp lemon juice
1 tsp Dijon mustard
175ml (6fl oz) sunflower oil
50ml (2fl oz) olive oil
Salt and freshly ground black pepper

First make the aïoli. Place the garlic in a bowl with the egg yolks, lemon juice and mustard. Mix both oils in a jug and, whisking constantly, pour them slowly into the egg yolk mixture in a very thin stream. Continue to add the oil, whisking all the time until it has been fully incorporated and the aïoli is thick. Season with salt and pepper to taste and set aside.

Slice the rolls in half and toast them on each side, then spread with butter and a little of the aïoli. Assemble the lamb, cucumber, red onion, feta and salad leaves on top of one half of each roll, then sandwich together with the other half. Cut the filled rolls in half and serve.

✳ The aïoli can be made in advance and stored in the fridge for up to 12 hours.

⬁ Any leftover aïoli would be delicious served with chips.

RACHEL'S TIP To reheat the lamb, place in an ovenproof dish, cover with foil and leave in a moderate oven (preheated to 180°C/350°F/Gas mark 4) for 5–10 minutes or until warmed through.

LAMB AND PEARL BARLEY BROTH

A simple yet soothing soup that I find hugely restorative on cold and rainy evenings, this is a delicious way to make roast lamb (see page 146) go that little bit further. It uses pearl barley, which has long been added to soups and stews to bulk them up when meat was scarce. Pearl barley provides more than just bulk, however, its soft, yielding texture as welcome here as its delightfully nutty taste.

Serves 6

25g (1oz) butter

2 tbsp olive oil

2 onions, peeled and finely chopped

2 cloves of garlic, peeled and crushed
  or finely grated

2 sticks of celery, trimmed and finely chopped

1 bay leaf

1 sprig of rosemary

Salt and freshly ground black pepper

200g (7oz) cooked lamb (see page 146), sliced
  or shredded into roughly bite-sized pieces

1 parsnip, peeled and finely chopped

2 carrots, peeled and finely chopped

100g (3½oz) pearl barley or pearled spelt

1.25 litres (2 pints) chicken stock (see page 20)

2 tbsp chopped parsley

Place the butter and olive oil in a large saucepan on a medium heat. Once the butter is melted and foaming, add the onions, garlic, celery, bay leaf and rosemary. Season with salt and pepper, then turn the heat to low, cover with a lid and sweat gently for 5–8 minutes or until the onions are softened but not browned.

Add the lamb, parsnip, carrots, pearl barley or pearled spelt and the stock. Turn the heat up and simmer, with the lid on, for about 25 minutes or until the vegetables and barley are tender. Remove the bay leaf and rosemary and stir in the chopped parsley, then season with more salt and pepper to taste and serve.

✳ The soup can be made up to two days in advance, covered and stored in the fridge; reheat on the hob to serve. It can also be frozen for up to three months.

⊖ The quantities in this recipe can be halved or multiplied.

SHEPHERD'S PIE

An all-time classic, shepherd's pie must be the epitome of comforting home-cooked food. It has the added advantage that it can be prepared entirely in advance with leftover cooked lamb if you have some to hand, and kept either in the fridge or freezer until you're ready to cook. A dish that is as convenient as it is totally delicious.

Serves 4–6
25g (1oz) butter
2 onions, peeled and diced
2 cloves of garlic, peeled and crushed
    or finely grated
500g (1lb 2oz) raw minced lamb, or 500g (1lb 2oz)
    cooked lamb (see page 146), cut into roughly
    1cm (½in) pieces
25g (1oz) plain flour
500ml (18fl oz) chicken stock (see page 20)
1 tbsp tomato paste or purée
Salt and freshly ground black pepper
2 tbsp chopped chives
700g (1lb 9oz) mashed potato (see page 199)

Equipment
20 x 30cm (8 x 12in) ovenproof dish

Preheat the oven to 180°C (350°F), Gas mark 4.

Melt the butter in a saucepan on a medium heat and when it is foaming, add the onions and garlic and cook for 5 minutes or until soft but not browned. If using raw minced lamb, add it to the pan now and cook, stirring occasionally and breaking up with a wooden spoon, until no trace of pink remains.

Stir in the flour and cook for 1 minute, then add the stock and tomato paste or purée, bring to the boil and season with salt and pepper. If using raw lamb, turn the heat down to low and simmer for 10 minutes, then add the chopped chives. If using cooked lamb, simply stir in with the chives.

Pour the lamb and sauce into the ovenproof dish and top with the mashed potato, adding it in blobs, then carefully spreading it over the lamb mixture to cover. Place in the oven and bake for about 30 minutes or until bubbling hot and golden brown on top.

✳ Shepherd's pie can be prepared in advance up to the point of assembling it in the dish, then covered and stored in the fridge for a couple of days. Or it can be placed in the freezer, well covered, and kept for up to three months, then defrosted completely before being baked in the oven, as above.

Once baked, it can kept in the fridge for two days and reheated in a moderate oven (preheated to 180°C/350°F/Gas mark 4) for 30 minutes.

⊖ The quantities in this recipe can be halved or multiplied, depending on how many you're feeding.

SPICED LAMB GIGOT CHOPS

Cut from a shoulder of lamb, gigot chops have an ideal mix of fat, meat and bone for a fine-flavoured casserole. Also used in Irish stew, the gigot cut is relatively cheap but when cooked – as here – long and slowly, the meat is wonderfully tender. Marinated in a carefully balanced mixture of spices, the chops would go perfectly with Golden Couscous (see page 191) or the Saffron Rice with Sultanas and Pistachios (see page 190).

Serves 4

1 tbsp cumin seeds, toasted and ground (see tip below)
1 tbsp coriander seeds, toasted and ground (see tip below)
2 tsp smoked paprika
1 tsp sea salt
1 tsp freshly ground black pepper
100ml (3½fl oz) olive oil
4 x 350g (12oz) lamb gigot chops, cut 2cm (¾in) thick (ask your butcher to do this for you)
2 red onions, peeled and sliced
2 cloves of garlic, peeled and crushed or finely grated
1 x 400g tin of chopped tomatoes, or 400g (14oz) ripe tomatoes, peeled (see tip on page 128) and chopped
1 tsp sugar

In a bowl, mix together the spices, salt and pepper with 50ml (2fl oz) of the olive oil to form a paste. Cover the lamb chops with the spice mix and leave to marinate for 1 hour.

Meanwhile, preheat the oven to 150°C (300°F), Gas mark 2.

Pour the remaining oil into a casserole dish or ovenproof saucepan and place on a medium–high heat. When the oil is hot, add the lamb chops and cook for 1–2 minutes on each side or until golden, being careful not to burn the spice mix. Remove the lamb from the dish and place on a plate.

Add the onions and garlic to the casserole dish and cook for 4–5 minutes or until softened and a little golden. Tip in the tomatoes and add the sugar, then put the lamb back in the dish.

Bring the mixture to a simmer, then cover with a lid and place in the oven to cook for 1½ hours or until the meat is meltingly tender. Serve on its own or with rice or couscous (see introduction above), or even mashed potato (see page 199).

✳ This can be cooked up to two days in advance, then kept in the fridge and reheated gently on a low–medium heat when you're ready to serve.

⊖⁺ The quantities in this recipe can be halved or multiplied, depending on how many you're feeding.

RACHEL'S TIP Place both the cumin and the coriander seeds in a non-stick pan over a medium–high heat and cook for a minute or so, tossing once or twice, until slightly darker in colour and toasted. Tip the toasted seeds into a mortar and crush with a pestle until fine, or place in a plastic bag and crush with a rolling pin instead.

HAM & PORK

SLOW-ROAST PORK BELLY WITH ROSEMARY

This might be my favourite cut of pork. Though much of the fat is rendered and poured away during cooking, the meat remains quite fatty. But that's the whole point of pork belly! The fat not only has a divine texture and flavour of its own, it lubricates and moistens the meat. A few hours' cooking transforms this affordable cut of meat into an absolute feast. Serve with seasonal vegetables, Perfect Mashed Potato (see page 199), Roasted Broccoli (see page 204), Roasted Butternut Squash with Thyme (see page 213) or Root Vegetable Gratin (see page 219).

Serves 4–6

1.25kg (2¾lb) piece of pork belly, off the bone and with the rind still on
3 tbsp olive oil
2 tbsp chopped rosemary leaves
1 tsp cracked black peppercorns
1 tsp sea salt flakes

For the gravy

15g (½oz) butter
15g (½oz) plain flour
200ml (7fl oz) chicken or duck stock (see pages 20 and 21)
Salt and freshly ground black pepper

Preheat the oven to 140°C (275°F), Gas mark 1.

Ask your butcher to score the pork rind or do so yourself: Using a sharp small knife, score the rind from top to bottom, each line spaced 0.5–1cm (¼–½in) apart, cutting through the rind only and not into the meat, then place it in a roasting tin.

In a bowl, mix together the olive oil, rosemary, black pepper and salt. Rub the mixture into the pork, pressing it into the rind, the sides of the meat, and underneath. Leave the pork to marinate for at least 30 minutes, or up to 2 hours in the fridge.

Cook the pork in the oven for 3½–4 hours or until the meat is very tender. Turn the oven temperature up to 200°C (400°F), Gas mark 6, and cook the pork for another 20–40 minutes until the rind is golden and you have crunchy crackling.

Transfer to a warmed serving plate and let the pork sit somewhere warm (such as in the oven,

with the heat switched off and the door slightly ajar) for 20 minutes while you make the gravy.

First make the roux. Melt the butter in a small saucepan on a medium heat and stir in the flour. Cook, stirring frequently, for about 1 minute and then set aside.

Pour the fat in the roasting tin into a jar or bowl (see 🗁 below). Place the roasting tin on a medium heat and deglaze with a little of the stock, using a whisk to scrape any sticky bits from the bottom of the tin. If the liquid is still looking fatty, pour it into a bowl or jug and allow to cool for a few minutes (adding a few ice cubes will speed the process), by which time the fat will have floated to the top and can be scooped up with a spoon.

Pour the degreased juices into a saucepan with the rest of the stock and bring to the boil. Whisk in the roux a little at a time and continue to boil for 1–2 minutes to thicken to the desired consistency. Season to taste, then strain the gravy through a fine sieve into a warmed gravy boat or jug.

Carve the pork through the scored crackling and serve with the gravy.

(✳) Leftover cooked pork can be kept in the fridge for up to three days.

(🗁) The fat from the roast pork can be kept for a few months in the fridge and used for roasting potatoes.

Any leftover cooked pork can be used in salads or sandwiches, such as the Pork Sliders with Red Cabbage Salad (see page 163), or in the Ginger Pork Stir-fry (see page 164).

PORK SLIDERS WITH RED CABBAGE SALAD

It's rare to find better accompaniments than stuffing and apple sauce in a pork sandwich, but this recipe with its crisp cabbage salad must be on a par at least. It's important that the pork (leftover roast pork belly, see page 160, is ideal here) is warmed through first, to ensure that it's moist and has maximum flavour. The salad adds crispness, plus a juicy sharpness from the dressing and extra texture from the crunchy pecans.

Makes 8 sandwiches
8 bread rolls
400g (14oz) cooked pork belly (see page 160
  – use however much you have left over), pulled
  or cut into shreds, rind included

For the dressing
2 tbsp Dijon or wholegrain mustard
½ tsp sugar
4 tbsp olive oil
2 tbsp cider vinegar

For the red cabbage salad
¼ red cabbage, core removed and leaves
  finely shredded
2 eating apples, cored and cut into thin slices
½ red onion, peeled and thinly sliced
75g (3oz) shelled pecans, very coarsely chopped
Salt and freshly ground black pepper

First make the dressing, whisking together all the ingredients in a bowl. Tip all the ingredients for the cabbage salad into the bowl and mix together well to coat in the dressing, seasoning to taste with salt and pepper.

Cut the rolls in half and toast them on both sides, then place a large frying pan on a high heat and add the pork belly, stirring just to warm through.

To assemble the sandwiches, add a good spoonful of the salad to one half of each bread roll and top with a few forkfuls of pork belly. Add the top half to each roll and serve while still warm.

⊕ If you have more pork belly to spare, you can easily multiply the quantities in this recipe; it's well worth it as the filled rolls are a real crowd-pleaser.

GINGER PORK STIR-FRY

**A vibrant and speedy way to use up leftover pork belly (see page 160), this colourful
stir-fry demands seriously high heat: your frying pan (or ideally wok) must be hot
enough that the vegetables and meat will quickly sear and fry, rather than stew or boil.
It's therefore important that you have all the ingredients chopped and ready before you
start stir-frying. The ginger matchsticks, blanched and fried, give a touch
of spicy heat and added crunch.**

Serves 4

25g (1oz) root ginger, peeled and cut into thin
  matchsticks, and 1 tbsp finely grated root ginger
2 tbsp sunflower oil
200g (7oz) lean pork, such as pork fillet, or
  cooked pork belly (see page 160), trimmed
  and cut into roughly 5mm (¼in) slices
2 large cloves of garlic, peeled and crushed or
  finely grated
150g (5oz) carrots, peeled and finely sliced at
  an angle
150g (5oz) purple-sprouting broccoli or small
  broccoli florets
1 red or yellow pepper, deseeded and finely sliced
75g (3oz) kale leaves (stalks removed), shredded
2 tbsp sesame oil
1–2 tbsp soy sauce
3 tbsp roughly chopped coriander (leaves and
  fine stalks)

Place a small saucepan of water on a high heat
and bring to the boil, add the ginger and boil for
1 minute, then tip into a sieve and leave to drain.

Place a wok or large frying pan on a high
heat and allow it to get very hot. Before you
begin to stir-fry, make sure you have all the
ingredients prepared and ready as everything
is cooked very briefly and needs to be added
in quick succession.

When the wok or frying pan is smoking hot,
pour in the oil, then stir-fry the boiled ginger
for 30–60 seconds or until light golden. Remove
from the oil with a slotted spoon and leave to
drain on kitchen paper.

Immediately add the pork, garlic, grated
ginger and sliced carrots. Stir-fry for 2 minutes
or until the pork is cooked (if using raw pork)
and the carrots are beginning to soften around
the edges but still have a crunch in the centre,
then toss in the broccoli and peppers.

Continue to stir-fry for another minute
before adding the kale and tossing briefly:
10–20 seconds will be enough to wilt the kale.
Lastly, add the sesame oil, soy sauce (to taste)
and chopped coriander. Toss everything
together briefly and serve straight away with
rice or noodles.

⊘ Replace the pork with the same quantity of
leftover cooked turkey or chicken (see page 82).

SAUSAGE PASTA POT

This is the kind of quick, one-pot, storecupboard supper that I turn to when I want to save time on shopping, cooking and washing-up. The soothing combination of sausages, pasta and tomato sauce is no less delicious, even so.

Serves 4–6
25g (1oz) butter
1 tbsp olive oil
300g (11oz) onions, peeled and thinly sliced
Salt and freshly ground black pepper
400g (14oz) sausages, halved or quartered
2 x 400g tins of chopped tomatoes, or 800g (1¾lb) ripe tomatoes, peeled (see tip on p128) and chopped
1 tsp chopped thyme or rosemary leaves
300g (11oz) farfalle or other pasta, such as casarecce or fusilli (see tip below)
3 tsp sugar
125g (4½oz) grated cheese, such as Cheddar or Parmesan, to serve

Place a wide saucepan on a medium heat and add the butter and olive oil. When the butter is melted and foaming, add the onions, season with salt and pepper and cook, stirring regularly, until they are nearly softened and a little golden around the edges.

Tip in the sausages and cook, stirring every so often, for 4–5 minutes so that they get lightly browned all over. Add the tomatoes and chopped herbs and pour in 350ml (12 fl oz) of water. Turn up the heat to high and bring to the boil, then tip in the pasta. (It should be just covered in liquid; if not, add a little more water.)

Season with the sugar and salt and pepper to taste, then cover with a lid. Reduce the heat to low and cook for 12–15 minutes or until the pasta is tender but still has the tiniest bit of a bite. Check the pasta while it cooks to see that the sauce isn't drying out, and top up with water if needed.

When the pasta is cooked, take the pan off the heat. Taste for seasoning, adding more salt and pepper if necessary, and serve with grated cheese scattered over the top.

✳ This dish can be prepared in advance up to the point of adding the pasta, then stored in the fridge for up to two days. Reheat when you're ready to serve, adding the pasta as above.

⊕ The quantities in this recipe can be halved or multiplied, depending on how many you're feeding.

RACHEL'S TIP You can use leftover cooked pasta for this recipe, adding it after the tomatoes have been cooking for 10 minutes.

PORK SATAY WITH SPICY PEANUT SAUCE

Lean pork such as this always benefits from being marinated, and the highly aromatic mixture used here will ensure that the meat is particularly moist. But what really makes this dish is the spicy peanut sauce – a divine combination of ingredients that is at once sweet, spicy and sour. Try it on simply grilled pork or chicken.

Serves 4

450g (1lb) lean pork, such as pork fillet, trimmed and cut into 2cm (¾in) cubes

For the marinade

150ml (5fl oz) coconut milk
1 tbsp finely grated root ginger
1 tbsp finely chopped lemongrass
½ tsp ground turmeric
2 tsp freshly ground coriander seeds
2 tsp freshly ground cumin seeds
1 tsp freshly ground black pepper
1 tsp salt

For the spicy peanut sauce

3 generous tbsp crunchy peanut butter
½ fresh red chilli pepper, deseeded (optional) and chopped
2 cloves of garlic, peeled and crushed or finely grated
2 tsp finely grated root ginger
¼ tsp ground turmeric
1 generous tbsp honey
2 tbsp soy sauce
1 tbsp lemon juice

Equipment

Wooden satay sticks or metal skewers

In a large bowl, mix together all the ingredients for the marinade. Add the meat, turning it in the mixture to coat, and set aside for at least 1 hour or leave in the fridge for up to 24 hours.

While the meat is marinating, soak the wooden satay sticks (if using) in cold water for 30 minutes to prevent them from burning during cooking.

Next make the spicy peanut sauce. Place all the ingredients in a blender or food processor, add 50ml (2fl oz) of water and whiz until smooth.

When you are ready to cook the pork, thread the meat onto the wooden satay sticks or metal skewers.

Place a griddle pan or large, heavy-based frying pan on a medium–high heat until very hot, or allow the grill or barbecue to heat up. Place the pork on the satay sticks/skewers in the pan, under the grill or on the barbecue and cook for 3–4 minutes on each side or until no trace of pink remains inside the meat. Serve immediately with the spicy peanut sauce.

✳ The peanut sauce be made in advance and will keep in the fridge for up to a week.

LISTY'S GLAZED HAM

Listy is a friend of ours who is well known for her glazed ham that feeds a crowd,
be it for family at Christmas or for a gathering of friends. This is so good I never mind
having lots left over. In fact, I deliberately buy a bigger ham than I need as the leftovers
can be transformed into a number of delicious dishes, not to mention sliced cold for
sandwiches or to eat with a salad.

Serves at least 20 people

1 x 6.8–9kg (15–20lb) ham on the bone
  (see tip below), rind still on
About 40 cloves
500g (1lb 2oz) demerara sugar

Place the ham in a large pot of cold water and leave
it to soak overnight. The following day, drain the
soaking water, then cover in fresh cold water and
place the pot on a high heat. Bring to the boil and
then reduce the heat to low and leave to simmer for
7–8 hours, topping up with water if necessary, until
the ham is cooked. Alternatively, place in the oven
(preheated to 110°C/225°F/Gas mark ¼, or the
lowest setting) and cook for the same length of time.
(Listy always transfers the pot into the simmering
oven of her Aga.)

You can tell the ham is cooked when a piece
of the rind comes away easily from the fat. Also a
skewer inserted into the meat will come out easily.
Drain the ham (reserving the cooking water – see
⌂) and place in a roasting tin.

Preheat the oven (or raise the oven temperature
if it's already switched on) to 220°C (425°F), Gas
mark 7.

Pull the rind off the ham and discard it, then
score the fat with a knife in a grid pattern to make
squares or diamonds with lines roughly 2cm (¾in)
apart. Stick a clove into each square or diamond,
pushing it right into the fat with your thumb.
Next take about 400g (14oz) of the sugar and
pack it onto the fat, pressing it in with your hands.

Place in the oven and cook for 30–50 minutes
or until the sugar coating is deep golden and
caramelised. Halfway through the cooking time,
take the ham out to baste it and add the
remaining sugar.

✳ The ham can be cooked in advance and stored
in the fridge, well wrapped, for up to four days.

⌂ Reserve the ham-cooking water for making
minestrone (see page 174).

Cooked ham is endlessly versatile, so any
leftovers can be put to good use – in salads,
sandwiches or included in other dishes, such as
minestrone, Chicken and Ham Pie (see page 89)
and Tartiflette (see page 177).

RACHEL'S TIP Ask your butcher to take out the shank and the aitchbone. Removing,
or at least 'cracking', the shank will allow you to squash the ham into a smaller pot than
otherwise. With the aitchbone removed, the cooked ham will be much easier to carve too.

MINESTRONE

Minestrone means 'big soup'. There are hundreds of different versions of this rustic soup for all seasons, which is exactly what it is: a soup that you can make with whatever vegetables happen to be at their seasonal best. I've used borlotti beans but would happily substitute with cannellini beans or butter beans. I love using risotto rice, for its almost creamy texture, but you could use broken-up spaghetti or small pasta shapes instead. I have given a winter and a summer variation of this recipe, but feel free to add whatever vegetables you like. Leftover ham-cooking water (see page 171) is just too good to waste, so I've used it here, along with leftover ham, but this soup is equally good without meat – just use vegetable stock or even water and omit the cubes of ham.

Serves 6

25ml (1fl oz) olive oil, plus extra for drizzling
1 medium–large onion, peeled and diced
1 clove of garlic, peeled and crushed
   or finely grated
3 carrots, peeled and diced
3 sticks of celery, trimmed and diced
Salt and freshly ground black pepper
1.75 litres (3 pints) ham-cooking water (see page
   171) or vegetable or chicken stock (see page 20)
1 small bay leaf
225g (8oz) risotto rice, such as Arborio
½ x 400g tin of borlotti beans (or cannellini
   or butter beans), drained and rinsed, or 100g
   (3½oz) dried borlotti beans (or cannellini
   or butter beans), soaked and cooked (see tip
   below)
275g (10oz) cooked ham (see page 171), cut into
   5mm (¼in) cubes
60g (2½oz) Parmesan cheese, grated, to serve

For summer minestrone

4 tomatoes, deseeded and diced
1 small courgette (about 10cm/4in long),
   trimmed and diced
75g (3oz) fresh or frozen peas or small broad beans

For winter minestrone

2 potatoes, peeled and diced
1 parsnip, peeled, quartered (tough core
   removed) and cubed
75g (3oz) kale leaves (stalks removed), such
   as cavolo nero, shredded

Place a large saucepan on a medium heat and add the olive oil. When the oil is hot, add the onion, garlic, carrots and celery and season with salt and pepper. Reduce the heat to low, then cover with a lid and sweat for about 8 minutes, stirring occasionally, until the vegetables are soft but not browned.

Pour in the ham-cooking water or stock and bring to the boil, then add the bay leaf, rice and the cooked borlotti beans and leave to simmer with the lid on the pan.

RACHEL'S TIP To cook the dried beans, first soak them in plenty of cold water overnight. Drain and place in a saucepan filled with fresh water. Place on a high heat and bring to the boil, then reduce the heat and simmer for ¾–1 hour or until tender. Remove from the heat, drain in a colander and allow to cool.

If making the summer minestrone, allow the mixture to simmer for 10 minutes, then add the ham, tomatoes and courgette and cook for another 2–3 minutes or until almost soft. Tip in the peas or broad beans and cook for a further 2 minutes, then remove from the heat.

If making the winter minestrone, let the mixture simmer for 5 minutes, then add the potatoes and parsnip and cook for another 5 minutes. Add the ham and cook for 5 minutes or until the potatoes and parsnips are almost soft. Stir in the kale and cook for a further 2–3 minutes or until wilted, then remove from the heat.

Taste the finished soup for seasoning, adding more salt and pepper if necessary. To serve, ladle into deep warmed bowls, drizzle liberally with olive oil and scatter some grated Parmesan over each.

✳ Once made, the soup can be stored in the fridge, where it will keep for a couple of days. Reheat gently to serve.

⊖⁺ You could happily halve or double the quantities in this recipe, though if halving I would still recommend using a whole clove of garlic.

TARTIFLETTE

Each valley in the Haute Savoie region in France seems to have its own recipe for tartiflette, all no doubt making use of the area's own Reblochon cheese. Here is my version of this wonderfully rich potato, onion and cheese gratin, which changes every time we make it at home, depending on what cheese we have in the fridge, or indeed what needs using up, such as leftovers from a roast ham (see page 171).

Serves 4–6

500g (1lb 2oz) potatoes, peeled, and halved
   if large, or cooked potatoes (see tip below)
Salt and freshly ground black pepper
1 tbsp olive oil (optional)
200g (7oz) rindless bacon or cooked ham (see
   page 171), cut into 0.5 x 2cm (¼ x ¾in) pieces
100g (3½oz) Cheddar cheese, or a mixture
   of Cheddar and Gruyère, grated
1 small shallot or 1 small red onion, peeled
   and finely sliced
1 clove of garlic, peeled and finely chopped
1 tsp chopped thyme leaves
200g (7oz) Camembert, or other semi-soft
   cheese, rind left on and cut into wedges
   (5mm/¼in at the thickest part)
200ml (7fl oz) single or regular cream

Equipment
25cm (10in) diameter ovenproof dish

First boil the potatoes (if cooking from scratch). Place the potatoes in a large saucepan, cover with water and add 1 teaspoon of salt. Bring to the boil and cook for 20–25 minutes or until tender, then remove from the heat. Drain and allow to cool a little before cutting into thick slices.

   To cook the bacon (if using), add the olive oil to a frying pan on a medium heat. When the oil is hot, tip in the bacon pieces and fry, stirring frequently, for 4–5 minutes or until lightly browned. Remove from the pan and set aside.

   Preheat the oven to 220°C (425°F), Gas mark 7.

   Arrange the potato slices on the base of the ovenproof dish, then scatter over the grated cheese with the sliced shallot or red onion, garlic and thyme. Next scatter over the cooked bacon or ham. Arrange the cheese wedges over the top, then pour over the cream and season with salt and pepper.

   Place in the oven to bake for 15–20 minutes or until golden and bubbling. Serve with a green salad if you wish.

(✳) This dish can be assembled in advance up to the point of baking and will keep, covered, in the fridge for up to 24 hours.

   Though best eaten straight away, any leftovers can be kept in the fridge and reheated again the next day in the oven (preheated to 180°C/350°F/ Gas mark 4) for 30 minutes or until hot.

(⊕) The quantities in this recipe can be easily halved or multiplied, depending on how many people you're feeding. If doubling quantities, use two dishes or one larger one, baking for a few extra minutes longer in the latter instance.

RACHEL'S TIP   Making tartiflette is a great way of using leftover cooked potatoes, whether boiled or roasted. If you have any lurking in the fridge, use these instead of cooking potatoes from scratch.

THAI PORK NOODLE SOUP

I've spent some time in Southeast Asia and some of the best dishes I sampled there were the broths – steaming in a big bowl, with their characteristic aromas of ginger and lemongrass. Salty, spicy, sharp and sweet, the flavours are strong yet always in balance with each other, and I've tried to recreate that in the recipe below. The ingredients are all easy to get hold of these days, from big supermarkets as well as specialist food shops, and the recipe itself is straightforward to prepare. The base of the soup is the flavourful broth, which would make a meal in itself with the noodles and maybe some extra greens. I can't resist these Asian-style meatballs, though, which should be properly browned to maximise their flavour before they're added to the broth.

Serves 4

100g (3½oz) medium or fine rice noodles

2 tbsp sunflower or rapeseed oil

½–1 fresh red chilli pepper, deseeded (optional) and finely chopped, to serve

For the broth

1 litre (1¾ pints) chicken stock (see page 20)

1 stalk of lemongrass, bashed (or rolled with a rolling pin) and halved

1 x 3cm (1¼in) piece of ginger, peeled and cut into about 6 slices

1 tbsp fish sauce (*nam pla*)

Juice of 1 lime

1 tbsp light soy sauce

2 tsp palm sugar or brown sugar

1–2 fresh red chilli peppers, deseeded (optional) and sliced

For the pork balls

Small bunch of coriander (about 20 stalks)

400g (14oz) lean minced pork

2 tsp finely grated root ginger

1 clove of garlic, peeled and crushed or finely grated

Salt

Place the noodles in a bowl, then cover with boiling water over and leave to stand for the length of time specified in the packet instructions or until softened. Drain the noodles in the colander, retaining about 50ml (2fl oz) of the soaking liquid, and tip the noodles back into the bowl with the reserved liquid.

Next make the broth. Pour the stock into a large saucepan, add the lemongrass and ginger and place on a high heat. Bring to the boil, then reduce the heat to medium and simmer for 5 minutes. Add the remaining ingredients, then taste and add a splash more fish sauce or lime juice if necessary. Leave to simmer on a low heat while you prepare the pork balls.

To make the pork balls, first cut off the thick stems from the base of the coriander stalks (just 2–3cm/¾–1¼in of stalk) and discard. Pick the coriander leaves off the remaining stems and set aside, then finely chop the stems.

In a bowl, mix the minced pork with the ginger, garlic and coriander stems and season with salt. To check the seasoning, cook a little piece of the mixture in the frying pan, then taste, adding more salt if necessary.

Roll the mixture into 20 balls, each the size of a walnut in its shell. Place a large frying pan on a high heat and allow it to get hot before adding the sunflower or rapeseed oil. Tip in the pork balls, or as many as will fit comfortably in a single layer. (You may have to cook them in two batches, adding more oil as needed.) Fry, stirring occasionally, for 6–8 minutes or until cooked in the centre and golden brown all over, then remove from the pan with a slotted spoon and transfer to a large plate lined with kitchen paper to drain.

Divide the noodles between four warmed bowls, then add the pork balls and pour over the broth, leaving the ginger slices and lemongrass in the saucepan. Garnish with the reserved coriander leaves and finely chopped chilli and serve immediately.

(✳) You could make the pork balls ahead of time (without frying them) and keep either in the fridge for up to two days or in the freezer for up to three months. Allow to defrost before cooking and serving as per method on left.

(⊕) The quantities in this recipe can be easily halved or doubled.

PULSES, GRAINS & PASTA

MOROCCAN CHICKPEA TAGINE

Moroccan cooking uses careful spice combinations to make dishes irresistibly aromatic. The recipe here follows the same principles to make a hugely flavoursome tagine, but don't be put off by the long list of ingredients. It won't take much of your time and makes for an impressive vegetarian meal. The nutty softness of the chickpeas is offset by the sweet dried fruit and crunchy flaked almonds, with cooling yoghurt to counterbalance the spice in the dish.

Serves 4–6

3 tbsp olive oil

1 large onion (about 300g/11oz), peeled and finely chopped

2 cloves of garlic, peeled and crushed or finely grated

½ tbsp smoked paprika

½ tbsp ground ginger

½ tbsp ground turmeric

½ tbsp ground cinnamon

Salt and freshly ground black pepper

2 x 400g tins of cooked chickpeas, drained and rinsed, or 250g (9oz) dried chickpeas, soaked overnight and cooked (see tip below)

50g (2oz) dried apricots, halved

50g (2oz) pitted dates, halved

Large pinch of saffron threads, soaked in 2 tbsp boiling water

2 x 400g tins of chopped tomatoes, or 800g (1¾lb) ripe tomatoes, peeled (see tip below) and chopped

2 tbsp honey

100g (3½oz) baby spinach leaves

To serve

2 handfuls of coriander leaves

100g (3½oz) flaked almonds, toasted (see tip below)

Lemon or lime wedges

250g (9oz) thick natural yoghurt, such as Greek yoghurt

Pour the oil into a large saucepan or casserole dish and place over a medium heat. Add the onion and garlic and fry, stirring occasionally, for about 10 minutes or until completely softened and a little golden around the edges. Stir in the ground spices with 1 teaspoon of black pepper and 2 teaspoons of salt and cook for a further 2 minutes.

Next add the chickpeas, apricots and dates, followed by the saffron (with its soaking liquid), tomatoes and honey. Pour in 300ml (½ pint) of

RACHEL'S TIPS To cook the dried chickpeas, first soak them in plenty of cold water overnight. Drain and place in a saucepan filled with fresh water. Place on a high heat and bring to the boil, then reduce the heat and simmer for ¾–1 hour or until tender. Remove from the heat, drain in a colander and allow to cool.

To peel the tomatoes, use a sharp knife to score a cross in the base of each one, cutting through the skin. Place the tomatoes in a bowl and cover with boiling water, leaving them in the water for 15–20 seconds. Drain and rinse in cold water, then peel away the skin – it should come away very easily.

To toast the flaked almonds, tip into a non-stick frying pan and toast over a high heat for a minute or two, tossing regularly to avoid burning. Take off the heat and set aside to cool.

water and bring to a simmer, then reduce the heat to low, cover with a lid and simmer gently for 45 minutes, stirring occasionally. Remove the lid and continue to cook for 10–15 minutes or until much of the liquid has evaporated and the mixture is quite thick.

Stir in the spinach and cook for just 1 minute or until the leaves have wilted, then remove from the heat. Taste for seasoning, adding more salt and pepper if needed, then divide between plates, scatter with the coriander leaves and toasted flaked almonds, and serve with the wedges of lemon or lime and a blob of thick yoghurt.

(✳) If you want to make this in advance, it will be perfect – even better, in fact – the following day or two days after you've cooked it. For the best results, add the spinach leaves to the reheated dish just before serving and cook for 1 minute. Having said that, if you have any left over, with the spinach leaves already in, it will still keep for up to three days – just reheat gently to serve. It can also be frozen for up to three months.

NUTTY QUINOA SALAD

✳ ⊖ ⊡

Grain-like quinoa (in fact, a seed) is as filling as it is reassuringly nutritious. It makes an ideal basis for salads, as it happily accommodates other ingredients while providing its own nutty flavour and lightly resistant texture. Without parsley leaves, this is the perfect salad for picnics or packed lunches as it will be just as good hours after making.

Serves 4 as a light lunch

1 small butternut squash (about 500g/1lb 2oz), peeled, deseeded and cut into roughly 3cm (1¼in) chunks, or ½ quantity of Roasted Butternut Squash with Thyme (see page 213)
10 sprigs of thyme
50ml (2fl oz) olive oil
Salt and freshly ground black pepper
50g (2oz) whole almonds (with their skins on)
250ml (9fl oz) water or vegetable or chicken stock (see page 20)
125g (4½oz) quinoa
100g (3½oz) feta cheese, crumbled into roughly 1cm (½in) chunks
4 tbsp chopped parsley

Preheat the oven to 200°C (400°F), Gas mark 6.

If cooking the squash from scratch, place in a roasting tin and add the thyme and olive oil. Mix together, season with salt and pepper, then place in the oven and roast for 30–40 minutes or until tender and slightly caramelised around the edges. Remove from the oven and set aside. Alternatively, take the previously roasted squash (if using) out of the fridge to bring it up to room temperature.

While the squash is cooking, scatter the almonds on a baking tray and place in the oven to roast for 5 minutes, tossing halfway through. Remove the nuts from the oven and chop very roughly with a knife.

Meanwhile, pour the water or stock into a saucepan on a medium heat and bring to the boil. Add the quinoa and some salt and pepper, then reduce the heat to low, cover with a lid and cook for 10–12 minutes or until all the liquid has been absorbed and the quinoa is just tender.

When the quinoa is cooked, place in a large bowl with the roasted squash, chopped nuts, feta and parsley. Mix everything together, taste for seasoning, adding more salt and pepper if necessary, and serve either warm or at room temperature.

✳ You can make the salad in advance as it will keep, stored in the fridge, for 24 hours. Take it out of the fridge half an hour or so before serving to bring it up to room temperature.

⊖ The quantities in this recipe can be doubled to serve more people.

⊡ This salad is a perfect packed lunch or picnic dish (just remember to leave out the parsley leaves if you make it in advance).

MUSHROOM, THYME AND CHORIZO PENNE

⊘ ⊕

**Pasta with a creamy mushroom sauce is one of the staple suppers in our house.
The chorizo adds a lovely meaty bite and its warm spicy flavour, while the cream
is reduced to make it thick enough to coat the pasta and give a taste of luxury to
each forkful. This recipe uses button mushrooms, but you could equally use
oyster or wild mushrooms such as chanterelle.**

Serves 4

350g (12oz) penne or other pasta, such
   as conchiglie, farfalle or fusilli
2 tbsp olive oil
375g (13oz) button or other mushrooms,
   such as oyster or chanterelle, sliced
250g (9oz) chorizo, cut into roughly 5mm
   (¼in) slices
150ml (5fl oz) double or regular cream
150ml (5fl oz) chicken stock (see page 20)
1 tsp chopped thyme leaves
Salt and freshly ground black pepper
50g (2oz) Parmesan cheese, finely grated,
   to serve

Place a large saucepan of salted water on a high
heat and bring to the boil. Add the penne and
cook for the length of time specified in the
packet instructions or until the pasta is tender
but still has a little bite. Drain in a colander,
retaining 50ml (2fl oz) of the cooking liquid,

then tip the pasta back into the pan with the
reserved liquid.

While the penne is cooking, place a large frying
pan on a high heat. Add the oil and when it is hot,
tip in the mushrooms. Cook, stirring occasionally,
for 3–4 minutes or until wilted and lightly golden.

Add the chorizo and cook for a further 1–2
minutes, then stir in the cream, stock and chopped
thyme, season with salt and pepper and reduce the
heat to medium–low so the sauce is just bubbling.

Add the drained pasta and reserved cooking
water to the sauce, stirring to mix well, then
divide between individual bowls and serve with
some grated Parmesan over the top.

⊘ **Mushroom and thyme penne:** For a vegetarian
version of this dish, simply omit the chorizo and
use vegetable stock instead.

⊕ The quantities in this recipe can easily be
doubled to serve more people.

CONCHIGLIE WITH BROAD BEANS, COURGETTES AND CREAM

When fresh ingredients are in season and at their peak, cooking fabulous dishes is just so easy. The combination here of the sweet broad beans, lightly browned courgettes and peppery basil is irresistible. Add a little cream to bring everything together, some Parmesan to heighten the flavour and a squeeze of lemon to offset it all. I can think of few better recipes with which to celebrate summer.

Serves 4–6

400g (14oz) fresh (pods removed) or frozen broad beans

300g (11oz) conchiglie or other pasta, such as casarecce, farfalle or fusilli

2 tbsp olive oil

400g (14oz) courgettes (the smaller the better), cut at an angle into roughly 1cm (½in) slices

Salt and freshly ground black pepper

200ml (7fl oz) double or regular cream

4 tbsp finely sliced basil

4 tbsp finely grated Parmesan cheese

Squeeze of lemon juice

Place a large saucepan of salted water on a high heat and bring to the boil. Add the broad beans, bring back up to the boil and cook for just 1 minute, then lift out with a slotted spoon and allow to cool, keeping the water in the pan for cooking the pasta. When the beans are cool enough to handle, pop them out of their skins and set aside in a bowl, discarding the skins.

Place the saucepan of salted water back on a high heat. When the water is boiling, add the conchiglie, then bring back up to the boil and cook for the length of time specified in the packet instructions or until just al dente. Drain in a colander, retaining 50ml (2fl oz) of the cooking liquid, then tip the pasta back into the pan with the reserved liquid.

As the pasta cooks, place a large frying pan on a medium–high heat. Add the olive oil and when it is hot, tip in the courgettes, season with salt and pepper and cook for about 2 minutes, tossing frequently, until lightly browned but still with a little bite.

Pour in the cream and allow to bubble for a couple of minutes until thickened, then remove from the heat and stir the cooked broad beans and pasta into the sauce with the basil and Parmesan. Taste for seasoning, add a squeeze of lemon and serve immediately.

The quantities in this recipe can be halved or multiplied.

SAFFRON RICE WITH SULTANAS AND PISTACHIOS

Adding just a few aromatics to rice elevates it into a truly special dish full of the enticing fragrances of the Middle East. This is the ideal partner for grilled or stewed lamb, such as the Spiced Lamb Gigot Chops (see page 157).

Serves 3–4 as a side dish
50g (2oz) butter
½ cinnamon stick
5 green cardamom pods
200g (7oz) basmati rice, rinsed
2 tbsp roughly chopped pistachios
2 tbsp sultanas
Salt
Good pinch of saffron threads, soaked
   in 4 tbsp boiling water

Melt the butter in a saucepan on a medium heat. When it has melted, stir in the cinnamon stick and cardamom. Fry, stirring occasionally, for about 2 minutes or until fragrant, then stir in the rice, pistachios and sultanas. Pour in enough water to cover the rice mixture by 1cm (½in), season with salt and place a lid on the pan. Bring to the boil, reduce the heat and cook for 10–15 minutes or until the rice is al dente, then stir in the saffron with its soaking liquid. Taste for seasoning, and serve immediately.

The quantities in this recipe can be halved or multiplied, if you wish.

PILAF RICE

This simple pilaf is a perfect accompaniment for Chicken and Bacon Casserole (see page 96), Quick Chicken Casserole (see page 86) or Spiced Lamb Gigot Chops (see page 157).

Serves 4–6 as a side dish
25g (1oz) butter
1 onion or 2 shallots, peeled and finely chopped
Salt and freshly ground black pepper
300g (11oz) basmati rice, rinsed
750ml (1⅓ pints) vegetable or chicken stock
   (see page 20)

Preheat the oven (if not cooking the rice on the hob) to 170°C (325°F), Gas mark 3. Melt the butter in a saucepan (ovenproof if necessary) or casserole dish. When it is foaming, add the onion or shallots, season, cover, reduce the heat and sweat for 8–10 minutes or until the onion is soft but not browned. Add the rice, stir on the heat for 2 minutes, then pour in the stock and season again. Bring to the boil, cover and simmer on the hob, or oven-bake, for 10 minutes or until the rice is just cooked and the liquid has been absorbed. Serve.

Try adding whole green cardamom pods, cinnamon sticks with the onion/shallots (remember to remove them before serving), or stirring in chopped parsley or dill at the end of cooking.

GOLDEN COUSCOUS

Couscous makes a wonderful accompaniment to any dish with a sauce, which it will soak up beautifully, and goes especially well with spiced lamb; the Lamb Kofta Tagine (see page 142), Lamb Neck with Yoghurt, Cucumber and Mint (see page 145) or Spiced Lamb Gigot Chops (see page 157) would be perfect. Made with good-quality stock, the couscous in this recipe is full of flavour and takes on a lovely golden colour from the turmeric.

Serves 3–4 as a side dish
25g (1oz) butter
1 onion, peeled and finely chopped
Salt and freshly ground black pepper
½ tsp ground turmeric
150g (5oz) couscous
2 tbsp olive oil
175ml (6fl oz) vegetable or chicken stock (see page 20)
Juice ½ lemon
75g (3oz) pine nuts, toasted (see tip below)

Melt the butter in a saucepan on a medium heat, then tip in the onion, season with salt and pepper and cook for 10–15 minutes or until softened and golden. Stir in the turmeric, then remove from the heat and set aside.

Meanwhile, place the couscous in a bowl and rub in the olive oil with your fingertips.

Pour the stock into another saucepan and bring to the boil, then pour over the couscous, cover the bowl with a plate or saucepan lid and allow to sit, somewhere warm, for 5–6 minutes or until the couscous has absorbed the stock.

Stir in the cooked onions, lemon juice and toasted pine nuts and season with salt and pepper to taste.

⊖⊕ The quantities in this recipe can be halved or doubled.

RACHEL'S TIP To toast the pine nuts, place in a non-stick pan over a medium–high heat and cook for a minute or so, tossing once or twice, until slightly darker in colour and toasted.

PICKLED BEETROOT, SWEET POTATO AND LENTIL SALAD

As nutritious as it is filling, this powerhouse of a salad is packed with different flavours – sharp, strong and sweet. With no leaves the salad can be kept after dressing for at least a day and so would make a perfect packed lunch.

Serves 3–4

2 sweet potatoes (about 600g/1lb 5oz total weight), peeled and cut into roughly 2cm (¾in) cubes
5 tbsp olive oil
Salt and freshly ground black pepper
150g (5oz) Puy or other brown lentils
1 tbsp red wine vinegar
100g (3½oz) pickled beetroot, cut into roughly 2cm (¾in) cubes
100g (3½oz) feta cheese, cut roughly into roughly 2cm (¾in) cubes
Good handful of chopped parsley, to serve

Preheat the oven to 200°C (400°F), Gas mark 6. Place the sweet potatoes in a bowl, then add 2 tablespoons of olive oil, season with salt and pepper and mix well. Transfer to a roasting tin and roast in the oven for 25–30 minutes, tossing occasionally, until soft and golden. Remove from the oven and set aside.

While the sweet potatoes are roasting, cook the lentils. Place in a saucepan and fill with enough water to cover the lentils by 2cm (¾in). Place on a high heat and bring to the boil, then reduce the heat and simmer, loosely covered with a lid, for 15–20 minutes or until the lentils are tender.

While the lentils are cooking, mix together 3 tablespoons of olive oil with the red wine vinegar and some salt and pepper to make a dressing. Drain the cooked lentils and while they are still warm, stir in two-thirds of the dressing and taste for seasoning.

To assemble the salad, spread the dressed lentils on a serving plate, then scatter over the roasted sweet potatoes along with the cubes of pickled beetroot and feta cheese. Drizzle over the remaining dressing and sprinkle with the chopped parsley, then serve either warm or at room temperature.

✳ This dish is best eaten on the day it's made, but any leftovers can be eaten within a day or two.

⊖⊕ The quantities in this recipe can be halved or multiplied.

▢ Leftovers are perfect for a packed lunch or picnic (just remember to leave out the herbs until you serve, if making it in advance).

RED LENTIL SOUP WITH CUMIN AND CORIANDER

✳ ⊖

The amount of flavour in the humble red lentil never fails to impress me. Not only are they astonishingly cheap, you need only a small amount to make a healthy portion of soup and they take less than 15 minutes to cook! This recipe has added support from the spices, onions and lemon, but it is the lentils' distinctive and delicious flavour that characterises this dish.

Serves 4

3 tbsp olive oil
1 onion, peeled and finely chopped
1 clove of garlic, peeled and crushed
   or finely grated
Salt and freshly ground black pepper
1 tsp cumin seeds, toasted and ground
   (see tip below)
1 tsp coriander seeds, toasted and ground
   (see tip below)
150g (5oz) split red lentils, rinsed
1 litre (1¾ pints) vegetable or chicken stock
   (see page 20)
Juice of ½ lemon
2 tbsp chopped coriander, mint or parsley

Place the olive oil in a large saucepan on a medium heat, add the onion, garlic and some salt and pepper, then cook, uncovered, for about 8–10 minutes or until the onion is slightly golden around the edges.

Add the ground spices and lentils and stir over the heat for 1 minute, then pour in the stock. Bring to the boil, then reduce the heat and simmer or 10–12 minutes or until the lentils have completely softened. Remove from the heat and add the lemon juice, stir in the chopped herbs and sprinkle over a little more salt if necessary.

✳ This can be made ahead of time as it keeps very well – in the fridge for up to three days or in the freezer for up to three months. Heat through and add the herbs just before serving.

⊖ The quantities in this recipe can be multiplied or halved very easily.

RACHEL'S TIP Place both the cumin and the coriander seeds in a non-stick pan over a medium–high heat and cook for a minute or so, tossing once or twice, until slightly darker in colour and toasted. Tip the toasted seeds into a mortar and crush with a pestle until fine, or place in a plastic bag and crush with a rolling pin instead.

VEGETABLES

SESAME PAK CHOI

Long eaten in Asia, pak choi has become popular in Ireland and the UK in recent years. In this recipe, the stems are separated from the leaves as the latter take only seconds to cook. Pak choi, with its fresh watery crunch, works so well with the sweet, nutty flavour of sesame, included here both as seeds and oil. I could – and often do – eat just a big bowl of this, but it's also great with fish, such as the Sunshine Fish Curry (see page 57), or with meat, such as the Duck Plum Spring Rolls (see page 111).

Serves 4 as a side dish

500g (1lb 2oz) pak choi
Salt
25g (1oz) sesame seeds, toasted (see
   tip below)
15ml (½fl oz) sesame oil

Remove the stems from the pack choi and cut them into lengths of a similar size (about 8cm/3in).

Bring a large saucepan of salted water to the boil. Add the pak choi stems and cook for 1–2 minutes or until just tender, then stir in the leaves and drain immediately.

Place in a serving dish, sprinkle over the toasted sesame seeds and sesame oil and serve immediately.

Use any leftovers for adding to the Chinese-style Duck Soup (see page 108).

RACHEL'S TIP To toast the sesame seeds, place in a non-stick pan over a medium–high heat and cook for a minute or so, tossing once or twice, until slightly darker in colour and toasted.

PERFECT MASHED POTATO

There are times when nothing else will do but fluffy, creamy and buttery mashed potato. One of the most comforting foods there is, it forms the backbone of countless meals and individual dishes (see ⊘ Pie Topping below). It's best to use a 'floury' variety, such as Golden Wonder or Kerr's Pink, for making mashed potato. For maximum goodness and flavour, peel the potatoes after boiling. (Floury potatoes tend to disintegrate, in any case, if you peel them beforehand.)

Makes about 1kg (2lb 3oz)/Serves 4 as a side dish
1kg (2lb 3oz) unpeeled floury potatoes, scrubbed clean
Salt and freshly ground black pepper
150ml (5fl oz) milk, or 110ml (4fl oz) milk and 50ml (2fl oz) single or regular cream
25g (1oz) butter

Place the potatoes in a large saucepan of salted water and bring to the boil. Boil for 10 minutes, then pour out all but 4cm (1½in) of the water, reduce the heat to very low and continue cooking the potatoes for another 20–30 minutes or until a skewer or sharp knife goes in easily. (Don't be tempted to stick a knife into the potatoes while they cook as the skins will break and they will disintegrate.)

Drain the potatoes and peel while they are still hot, using a clean tea towel to protect your hands. Place the peeled potatoes in a large bowl and mash by hand until they are free of lumps. Alternatively, place in an electric food mixer and use the paddle attachment to mash them.

Pour the milk (or milk and cream) into a small saucepan and bring to the boil. Mix the butter in with the potatoes, seasoning with salt and pepper to taste, then add the boiling milk/cream and stir to a smooth consistency.

(You might not need all the milk/cream or you might need a little more – it depends on how dry the potatoes are.) Taste and adjust the seasoning if needed, then serve immediately or return the mash to a saucepan for reheating if not eating straight away.

⊘ **Pie topping:** The mash here can be made up to use on top of Chicken and Ham Pie (see page 89), Shepherd's Pie (see page 154) and Smoked Haddock Pie (see page 63). If I'm making mashed potato for this purpose, then I like to add a beaten egg to the mix at the same time as the milk. The egg yolk will cause the potato topping to turn slightly golden in the oven. Just bear in mind that you may not need as much milk if using the egg.

✳ If you make your mash in advance, add a little extra milk so it doesn't dry out as it sits. It will keep, covered, in a warm oven for an hour or so.

Mashed potato can sit in the fridge, covered, for up to two days when it can be reheated gently on the hob. You may need to add extra milk when reheating.

▣ Leftover mash is ideal for making Bubble and Squeak (see page 200) or Instant Cullen Skink (see page 64).

BUBBLE AND SQUEAK

Bubble and squeak originally came about as a tasty and ingenious way of using up leftovers from a roast dinner. And while this still holds true, bubble and squeak is so good, to my mind, that I often cook it from scratch. The recipe below uses crisp bacon, savoury leeks and aromatic herbs to delicious effect. You can, if you like, bulk it up into a more substantial supper by serving it with fried eggs.

Serves 6

45g (2oz) butter

2 small leeks or 1 medium–large leek, trimmed and thinly sliced

1 small savoy cabbage, cut into quarters, core removed and leaves thinly sliced

Salt and freshly ground black pepper

12 rashers of streaky bacon

800g (1¾lb) mashed potato (see page 199)

2 tbsp chopped mixed herbs, such as parsley and chives (optional)

6 eggs (optional)

Place a large frying pan on a high heat and add 15g (½oz) of the butter and 2 tablespoons of water. When the butter has melted and the water bubbling, tip in the leeks and cabbage. Season with salt and pepper and toss the vegetables together, stirring every so often. Cook until the cabbage is wilted, then tip into a large bowl.

Place the pan back on a high heat and add another 15g (½oz) of the butter. When the butter has melted, add the bacon rashers and fry for about 3 minutes or until golden on both sides.

Remove the bacon, retaining any fat in the pan, and place on kitchen paper to drain.

Add the mashed potato and the cabbage/leek mixture to the hot frying pan. Stir over the heat for 3–4 minutes and season with salt and pepper to taste. Add the herbs (if using), then serve immediately, with the crisp bacon rashers broken over the top, or tip into a warmed bowl and cover with a plate or saucepan lid to keep warm while you fry the eggs (if using).

Place the pan back over a high heat and add another 15g (½oz) of butter. When the butter has melted, break the eggs into the pan and fry until they are done to your liking. Divide the bubble and squeak between warmed plates, add a fried egg on top of each and scatter over broken-up bits of crisp bacon.

⊘ **Bubble and squeak cakes:** If you have any bubble and squeak left over, you could mould it into hamburger-sized patties. Dust these with flour and place in a medium-hot frying pan with a little olive oil and butter, then cook on either side for a few minutes until golden. These are also great topped with a fried egg and crispy bacon.

PANZANELLA

Panzanella is a classic Italian bread and tomato salad. Originally from Tuscany,
it is believed to have evolved from a rustic dish in which stale bread was soaked in water
before being mixed with tomatoes and other ingredients. Full of punchy Mediterranean
flavours, the version here is a meal in itself, although I also like serving it with
barbecued fish or meat. I love to use sherry vinegar in the dressing for its full complex
flavour, but if you can't find any then red wine vinegar would also work well.

Serves 4 as a side dish or light lunch

200g (7oz) crusty bread, cut or torn into roughly
  2cm (¾in) chunks

100ml (3½fl oz) olive oil

2 cloves of garlic, peeled and crushed
  or finely grated

Salt and freshly ground black pepper

1 cucumber, cut into roughly 2cm (¾in) dice

4 large tomatoes, cut into roughly 2cm (¾in) dice

1 red onion, peeled and cut into roughly 2cm
  (¾in) dice

1 red or yellow pepper, deseeded and cut into
  roughly 2cm (¾in) dice

75g (3oz) black olives, pitted and halved

50ml (2fl oz) sherry vinegar or red wine vinegar

200g (7oz) feta cheese, crumbled (optional)

Preheat the oven to 200°C (400°F), Gas mark 6.

Put the bread in a large bowl, add the olive oil and garlic and toss together, seasoning with salt and pepper. Place on a baking sheet and toast in the oven for 5 minutes or until golden and crispy, then remove from the oven and set aside.

In a large serving bowl, mix together the diced vegetables and the olives. Tip the toasted bread on top, then sprinkle over the vinegar and season with salt and pepper. Just before serving, top with the feta (if using) and serve.

※ The vegetables could be prepared a couple of hours in advance, if needed.

⊕ The quantities in this salad can easily be doubled.

ROASTED BROCCOLI

Roasting is a delightfully different way of cooking broccoli, which stays crunchy while gaining extra flavour from browning in the oven, the garlic adding sweetness and the pine nuts their distinctive texture. It can be served hot with grilled or cooked meats, especially lamb, or cold as a simple salad, either by itself or with other salads such as the Panzanella (see page 203) or Nutty Quinoa Salad (see page 185).

Serves 4 as a side dish

200g (7oz) broccoli, cut into florets
   (including the stalk)
50ml (2fl oz) olive oil
5 cloves of garlic, peeled and chopped
Salt and freshly ground black pepper
25g (1oz) pine nuts

Preheat the oven to 240°C (475°F), Gas mark 9, or its highest setting.

Place the broccoli florets in a bowl, add the olive oil and garlic and toss everything together, seasoning with salt and pepper. Tip into a roasting tin and place in the oven to cook for 10 minutes.

Remove from the oven, sprinkle over the pine nuts and return to the oven for a further 5 minutes or until the broccoli is slightly tender but still has a little bite and the pine nuts are golden. Remove from the oven and serve immediately.

Use any leftovers in Broccoli Orzo Salad (see below) and Chicken and Ham Pie (see page 89).

BROCCOLI ORZO SALAD

This is the sort of salad I love to throw together. It takes so little time but provides a wonderful array of contrasting textures and flavours. The orzo – pasta in the shape of large grains of rice – is perfect for this dish as it cooks very quickly being so small.

Serves 4–6

225g (8oz) orzo
150g (5oz) cherry tomatoes, quartered
200g (7oz) boiled or roasted broccoli
   (see above)
100g (3½oz) salami, thinly sliced
Juice of ½ lemon
3 tbsp olive oil
2 tbsp torn or sliced basil
50g (2oz) pine nuts, toasted (see tip on page 191)
Salt and freshly ground black pepper

Bring a saucepan of water to the boil. Add a pinch of salt and stir in the orzo, then cook for the length of time specified in the packet instructions or until al dente. Drain, retaining about 50ml (2fl oz) of the cooking water, then tip the orzo and reserved liquid back in the pan. Set aside and allow to cool to room temperature.

In a large bowl, toss together the orzo with the tomatoes, broccoli and salami. Drizzle over the lemon juice and olive oil, add the basil and season with salt and pepper to taste. Scatter with the toasted pine nuts and serve.

CHEESY KALE BAKE

I find a dish like this a good opportunity to use up any ends of cheese lurking in the fridge. Within reason, of course: the better the cheese, the better the dish will be, but a few different types of hard cheese mixed together is perfect. I prefer not to use blue cheese, however.

Serves 4

400g (14oz) curly kale (stalks removed),
    thickly shredded
25g (1oz) butter
25g (1oz) plain flour
400ml (14fl oz) milk
250g (9oz) Cheddar or Gruyère cheese
    (or mixed leftover hard cheese), grated
1 tsp Dijon mustard
Salt and freshly ground black pepper

Equipment

20 x 25cm (8 x 10in) ovenproof dish

Preheat the oven to 200°C (400°F), Gas mark 6.

Place a large pan of water on a high heat, add 1 teaspoon of salt and bring to the boil. Tip in the kale and cook for just a couple of minutes or until almost tender, then drain, squeezing the leaves to remove all the excess water, and place in the ovenproof dish.

To make the sauce, melt the butter in a saucepan over a medium heat, add the flour and cook for 1 minute or until bubbling. Gradually pour in the milk, whisking it into the flour and butter, and bring to the boil, then reduce the heat and cook for 3–4 minutes or until the sauce thickens. Remove from the heat, then add half the cheese and the mustard and season to taste with salt and pepper.

Pour the cheese sauce over the kale and sprinkle over the remaining cheese, then bake in the oven for 15–20 minutes or until bubbling and golden on top.

(✳) This can be prepared in advance right up until assembling in the dish and kept in the fridge for 24 hours, or it can be frozen for up to three months. Defrost fully before baking as above.

This dish will keep in the fridge for a couple of days once cooked. It's best served warm, reheated in the oven (preheated to 180°C/350°F/ Gas mark 4) for about 20 minutes to allow the cheese sauce to melt again.

(-+) You could halve or double the quantities in this recipe, using a dish of half/double the volume. It may take a few minutes less or longer to cook – just make sure it is bubbling and golden before removing from the oven.

STUFFED BUTTERNUT SQUASH WITH GOAT'S CHEESE

This stuffed squash makes for a fabulous and hearty meal. A larger squash will serve more than two people, but I think it can be quite special to have your whole meal presented in one edible vessel. The flavours of autumn here need no other accompaniment (though a glass of white wine wouldn't go amiss!).

Serves 2

1 large butternut squash (about 1kg/2lb 3oz)
1 tbsp olive oil
Salt and freshly ground black pepper
100g (3½oz) soft goat's cheese

For the stuffing

15g (½oz) butter
1 leek, tough green leaves trimmed and saved for stock or discarded, finely sliced (about 200g/7oz trimmed weight)
2 large flat mushrooms, chopped (about 150g/5oz total weight)
2 cloves of garlic, peeled and crushed or finely grated
1 tsp chopped thyme leaves

Preheat the oven to 200°C (400°F), Gas mark 6.

First cut the butternut squash in half lengthways. Remove the seeds, then use a teaspoon to scrape a channel about 1cm (½in) deep running down the neck of the squash. Discard this flesh along with the seeds and pulp.

Place the two halves of squash in a roasting tin and drizzle with the olive oil. Season with salt and pepper and place in the oven to roast for 20 minutes.

As the squash is roasting, make the stuffing. Melt the butter in a frying pan over a high heat, and when it is foaming, add the leek, mushrooms, garlic and thyme. Season with salt and pepper, then cook, stirring occasionally, for 8–10 minutes or until the vegetables have softened. Remove from the heat and set aside.

When the squash has cooked for 20 minutes, divide the mushroom and leek mixture between the squash halves, filling the bulb and scraped-out neck of the squash. Return to the oven and cook for a further 30 minutes.

After 30 minutes, crumble or slice the goat's cheese over the stuffing on the two squash halves. Return to the oven for about 15 minutes or until the goat's cheese is bubbling and lightly browned, then remove from the oven and serve immediately.

✳ The squash can be prepared and the leeks and mushrooms cut up an hour or so beforehand.

The stuffing can be cooked in advance and kept in the fridge overnight.

CRISPY SWEDE BAKE

Swede, like potato, is great for mashing. However, it has a tendency to become a little too moist, which is why I mash it back on the heat until it loses that excess moisture. The cream and butter provide the boost in richness the swede needs to make it the ideal wintertime accompaniment to roast meats such as turkey, chicken or lamb.

Serves 4–6 as a side dish
1 x 1.4kg (3lb) swede, peeled and cubed
4 cloves of garlic, peeled and slightly crushed
2 tbsp finely chopped chives
50ml (2fl oz) double or regular cream
25g (1oz) butter
Salt and freshly ground black pepper
25g (1oz) breadcrumbs (see tip below)

Equipment
20 x 30cm (8 x 12in) ovenproof dish

Preheat the oven to 200°C (400°F), Gas mark 6.

Fill a large saucepan with water and add a good pinch of salt, then place on a high heat and bring to the boil. Add the swede and garlic and simmer for 10–15 minutes or until soft. Drain in a colander, then return the swede and garlic to the pan and cook, while mashing them, for 2–3 minutes or until dry.

Remove the pan from the heat, then stir in the chives, cream and butter and season with salt and pepper. Tip into the ovenproof dish and scatter the breadcrumbs over the top. Place the mash in the oven and bake for 20 minutes or until bubbling hot and crisp and golden on top.

(✳) The mash can be prepared in advance (up to mixing in the cream and butter) and will keep, covered, in the fridge for up to 24 hours. Take out and bake as above.

After baking, this dish is best eaten straight away, but if you have some left over it can be kept (refrigerated) for up to two days, then popped back into a hot oven (preheated to 200°C/400°F/ Gas mark 6) to reheat for 20 minutes.

RACHEL'S TIP It is easy to make your own breadcrumbs from stale bread. If you have a food processor, tear the stale bread into piece and whiz for a few minutes to form breadcrumbs. If you don't have a food processor, tear the bread into pieces and place in a low oven for 10 minutes or so, until completely dry, then crush into breadcrumbs using a rolling pin. They keep well in the freezer in an airtight bag if you want to make them ahead of time.

SUMMER VEGETABLES WITH TARRAGON

Summer legumes such as these need only a little cooking to bring out their wonderful sweetness. A touch of richness from the crème fraîche and extra flavour from the tarragon are all that's wanted to produce a dish of real luxury. If you can't get hold of tarragon, you could use mint instead.

Serves 4 as a side dish
140g (5oz) French beans, topped and tailed
130g (4½oz) sugar snap peas
130g (4½oz) mangetout
100g (3½oz) crème fraîche
1 tbsp chopped tarragon
Salt and freshly ground black pepper

Place a large saucepan of salted water on a high heat and bring to the boil. Add the French beans and bring back up to the boil, then after 2 minutes add the sugar snap peas and bring back up to the boil once again before stirring in the mangetout. Drain immediately and tip into a warmed serving bowl.

Add the crème fraîche and tarragon to the empty saucepan, season with salt and pepper and warm through over a low–medium heat. Pour over the vegetables and serve.

This is best served and eaten straight away, but any leftovers will be delicious reheated briefly and tossed through freshly cooked pasta.

ROASTED BUTTERNUT SQUASH WITH THYME

I'm always impressed by the colossal size to which squash can grow in just one season. The butternut squash is not grown for its size, however, but for its soft moist flesh and incredible sweetness. An easy recipe, this dish would be happy as an accompaniment to roast meat. The whole roasted squash can also be used in the Thai Butternut Squash Soup (see page 215) and Roasted Butternut Squash Salad (see page 216).

Serves 4 as a side dish
1 large butternut squash (about 1kg/2lb 3oz), peeled, deseeded and cut into roughly 3cm (1¼in) chunks
10 small sprigs of thyme
50ml (2fl oz) olive oil
Salt and freshly ground black pepper

Preheat the oven to 200°C (400°F), Gas mark 6.

Spread the butternut squash chunks out on a large baking tray, then add the thyme sprigs, drizzle with the olive oil and season with salt and pepper.

Place in the oven and roast for 30–40 minutes or until completely tender and slightly caramelised around the edges.

✳ The cooked squash can be stored in the fridge for up to two days.

▢ Any leftover cooked squash could be used in the Nutty Quinoa Salad (see page 185).

THAI BUTTERNUT SQUASH SOUP

The squash (use Roasted Butternut Squash with Thyme, see page 213, if you have any left over) gives real body to this soup, making it a meal in a bowl. Its sweet taste provides the perfect foil for the dish's strong Southeast Asian flavours. This recipe can be made in advance, but don't add the basil until just before serving.

Serves 6

500ml (18fl oz) chicken stock (see page 20)
1 stick of lemongrass, crushed with a rolling pin
50ml (2fl oz) sunflower oil
1 large onion, peeled and diced
2 cloves of garlic, peeled and crushed
 or finely grated
1 fresh red chilli pepper, deseeded (optional)
 and diced
5cm (2in) piece of root ginger, peeled and grated
1 large butternut squash (about 1kg/2lb 3oz),
 peeled, deseeded and cut into roughly 3cm
 (1¼in) chunks, or 1 quantity of Roasted
 Butternut Squash with Thyme (see page 213)
Salt and freshly ground black pepper
1 x 400ml tin of coconut milk
1–2 tbsp fish sauce (*nam pla*)
Small bunch of basil, shredded (about 2 tbsp),
 to serve

Pour the chicken stock into a saucepan and add the lemongrass. Place on a medium heat and bring to a simmer, then remove from the heat and allow to infuse for at least 10 minutes.

Place a large saucepan on a high heat and add the sunflower oil. Add the onion, garlic, chilli, ginger and raw squash (if using), and season with salt and pepper. Turn the heat down to low, then cover with a lid and cook for about 10 minutes or until the squash is tender. Pour in the coconut milk and the hot chicken stock, including the lemongrass. Bring to the boil and cook, uncovered, for 5 minutes.

If using roasted butternut squash, add this with the coconut milk and stock and cook for 5 minutes.

Remove from the heat, then transfer to a blender and purée until smooth. Return the finished soup to the pan to heat through gently, then season with fish sauce to taste and serve sprinkled with the basil.

✳ The soup will keep, covered, in the fridge for up to three days; simply reheat to serve. It can also be frozen for up to three months.

ROASTED BUTTERNUT SQUASH SALAD

Leftover roast vegetables can be equally good served at room temperature, and squash is no exception. With just a few more ingredients, it makes a handsome meal. Packed full of nutrition, it also makes a great lunchbox meal. If you have time to make them (or have some left over), the flatbreads on page 27 would be lovely with this salad.

Serves 4–6

1 large butternut squash (about 1kg/2lb 3oz), peeled, deseeded and cut into 3cm (1¼in) pieces, or 1 quantity of Roasted Butternut Squash with Thyme (see page 213)

3 red onions, peeled and each cut lengthways into about 8 wedges

3 tbsp olive oil

10 small sprigs of thyme (if using raw squash)

Salt and freshly ground black pepper

1 tbsp balsamic vinegar or sherry vinegar

200g (7oz) mozzarella, torn into bite-sized chunks

50g (2oz) rocket leaves

25g (1oz) Parmesan cheese, grated

Preheat the oven to 200°C (400°F), Gas mark 6.

Place the raw squash (if using) and onion wedges in a roasting tin with the thyme sprigs and drizzle with 2 tablespoons of the olive oil. Season with salt and pepper and roast in the oven for 30–40 minutes or until completely tender and slightly caramelised around the edges.

Drizzle the vinegar over the warm vegetables and set aside to cool to room temperature. If using previously roasted squash, add it to the onions once they have cooled down.

When the vegetables have cooled, add the mozzarella and rocket and toss gently together. Sprinkle with grated Parmesan, then taste for seasoning, adding more salt and pepper if necessary, and serve.

Leftover roasted butternut squash salad makes a great packed lunch or picnic dish (just remember to leave out the rocket leaves if making it in advance, adding them just before serving).

ROOT VEGETABLE GRATIN

There is an open secret to making gratins taste divine – adding cream and plenty of it!
I like to combine carrots, parsnips and celeriac for their distinctive flavour and
contrasting colours. Serve as a rich accompaniment to roast chicken (see page 82)
or with grilled or roasted lamb; it would also make a delicious meal in itself.

Serves 6–8 as a side dish
600g (1lb 5oz) carrots, peeled
    (450g/1lb peeled weight)
600g (1lb 5oz) parsnips, peeled
    (450g/1lb peeled weight)
600g (1lb 5oz) celeriac, peeled
    (400g/14oz peeled weight)
500ml (18fl oz) double or regular cream
250ml (9fl oz) milk
3 cloves of garlic, peeled and crushed
    or finely grated
Salt and freshly ground black pepper
25g (1oz) butter, diced

Equipment
20 x 30cm (8 x 12in) ovenproof dish

Preheat the oven to 200°C (400°F), Gas mark 6.

Slice the carrots, parsnips and celeriac into bite-sized rounds or pieces about 3mm (⅛in) thick, then mix together in a large bowl.

Pour the cream and milk into a large saucepan and add the garlic. Place on a medium heat and bring to a simmer, then pour the hot liquid over the vegetables and mix together thoroughly. Season with salt and pepper and tip the mixture into the ovenproof dish. Cover with foil, then place in the oven to bake for 40 minutes.

Take the dish out of the oven and remove the foil. Dot the vegetables with the butter and bake for a further 20 minutes or until the vegetables are tender and golden on top. Remove from the oven and serve immediately.

SWEET THINGS

SUMMER FRUIT COMPOTE

I love that time in the summer when we're just spoilt for choice by all the soft fruit on offer, and this recipe takes full advantage of that. Compote is the best thing to have in your fridge for drizzling over ice cream, for instance, or serving with thick natural yoghurt for breakfast. You can substitute the berries with other kinds of fruit, if you prefer, and the compote can be incorporated in other desserts, such as the Summer Fruit Jelly (see page 225).

Serves 6–8

200g (7oz) caster sugar

1 vanilla pod

6 nectarines (about 700g/1lb 9oz total weight), stones removed and flesh cut into slices about 5mm (¼in) thick

300g (11oz) fresh strawberries, hulled and halved, or quartered if large

125g (4½oz) fresh or frozen blueberries

Juice of ½–1 lemon

Place the sugar and vanilla pod in a large saucepan, pour in 350ml (12fl oz) of water and set over a high heat. Cook the mixture, stirring occasionally, just until the sugar has dissolved.

Add the nectarine slices to the syrup. Bring to the boil, then reduce the heat to medium and leave to simmer for 6–8 minutes or until the nectarines are tender but still holding their shape, then remove from the heat and allow to cool.

Add the strawberries and blueberries and the lemon juice (to taste). Serve at room temperature or chilled. If you can let the compote sit for 1 hour for the flavours to mingle, then all the better, though it can be served straight away.

This is great eaten on its own, but it would be wonderful too with thick natural yoghurt, softly whipped cream or vanilla ice cream.

(✳) The nectarines can be poached in the syrup a day or two in advance, with the berries and lemon juice added closer to the time of serving.

The compote will keep, covered, in the fridge for up to two days.

(⊖+) The quantities in this recipe can be halved or multiplied easily. If you're doubling them up, there's no need to use two vanilla pods, however – you could split one down the side with a small knife.

(▱) Use any leftover syrup for making Summer Fruit Jelly (see page 225).

SUMMER FRUIT JELLY

This recipe is a great way to use up any leftover syrup from the Summer Fruit Compote (see page 222), although you could make the compote especially for the jelly, if you preferred. Once you've made the compote, drain the syrup for using in the jelly, and reserve the fruit for serving on top. Leftover syrup from poached fruit such as plums or rhubarb would work equally well otherwise. Serve with single cream poured over the top or (to release your inner child!) a dollop of ice cream.

Serves 3–4
300ml (½ pint) syrup drained from the Summer
   Fruit Compote (see page 222)
Lemon juice (optional)
2 tsp powdered gelatine or 2 sheets of
   leaf gelatine
Vegetable oil, for greasing

First taste the fruit syrup to make sure you're happy with the flavour. If it's too sweet add a little lemon juice.

If using powdered gelatine, place 2 tablespoons of cold water in a bowl or measuring jug and sprinkle in the gelatine. Place in the fridge for 5 minutes to 'sponge' (soak and swell) in the water. Meanwhile, fill a saucepan with a few centimetres of hot water, place on a low–medium heat and bring to a gentle simmer. When the gelatine has become sponge-like, sit the bowl or jug in the water for 4–5 minutes to

allow it to dissolve completely. Once dissolved, pour the fruit syrup into the gelatine and stir well to mix.

Pour the mixture into a large, greased bowl or several individual moulds, cups or glasses (also oiled). Place in the fridge for 3–4 hours to allow the jelly to set.

If using gelatine leaves, place these in a bowl and cover well with cold water. Leave to sit and soften for 5 minutes, then remove the softened leaves and place in another bowl. Add 2 tablespoons of boiling water and stir to dissolve, then pour in the fruit syrup and stir to mix before pouring into a greased bowl or moulds and placing in the fridge to set.

✳ The jelly will keep happily in the fridge for up to three days.

⊕ Double the quantities to serve 6–8.

ORANGE SWIRL LOAF

**Orange-flavoured butter adds a delightful citrusy sweetness to this white yeast dough.
The result is a beautiful loaf to tear apart and share – just perfect with a cup of coffee.**

Makes 1 loaf
1 tsp caster sugar
215ml (7fl oz) warm water
1½ tsp dried yeast or 15g (½oz) fresh yeast
    or 1 x 7g sachet fast-action yeast
350g (12oz) strong white flour, plus extra
    for dusting
1 tsp salt
15g (½oz) butter or 15ml (½fl oz) olive oil,
    plus extra for greasing
1 generous tbsp granulated sugar, for sprinkling

For the orange butter
75g (3oz) butter, softened
75g (3oz) icing sugar
Finely grated zest of 1 large orange

Equipment
23cm (9in) diameter baking tin

In a measuring jug, mix the caster sugar with the warm water and yeast and leave to stand in a warm place for 5 minutes or until the mixture is creamy. If using fast-action yeast, skip the standing time.

Sift the flour and salt into a large bowl, or the bowl of an electric food mixer fitted with a dough hook. Rub in the butter (if using) and make a well in the centre. (If using oil instead of butter, pour it into the yeast mixture.) Pour the yeast mixture (after adding the oil, if using) into the well and mix to a loose dough, adding more water if necessary.

Knead for about 10 minutes or until the dough is smooth and springy to the touch. (If kneading in the food mixer, 5 minutes is usually long enough.)

Grease the bowl with olive oil and put the dough back into it, then cover the top tightly with cling film and place somewhere warm to rise until the dough has doubled in size. This may take up to 2 hours or even up to 3 hours on a cold day.

As the dough rises, grease the baking tin and make the orange butter. In a separate bowl, beat together the butter, icing sugar and orange zest until thoroughly combined.

Transfer the risen dough to the worktop. Sprinkle the dough and the worktop with flour, then roll it out into a rectangle measuring 20 x 30cm (8 x 12in) and 3–4mm (⅛in) thick.

Place about 1 tablespoon of the orange butter in a small bowl and set aside for later. Spread the remaining orange butter over the rolled-out dough to cover it. Then, using both hands and starting at one of the long ends, roll up the dough (not too tightly) so that it resembles a Swiss roll. Using a sharp knife (serrated if possible) that you have dusted with flour, cut the loaf/roll into eight slices, each about 3.5cm (1½in) thick.

Arrange seven of these slices, cut side up, around the side of the tin and one in the middle, again cut side up. Brush or spread the reserved tablespoon of orange butter over the dough in the tin and sprinkle with the granulated sugar. The gaps between the swirls will close as the dough proves.

Set aside and leave to prove in a warm place for about 30 minutes or until doubled in size. There is no need to cover the tin with a tea towel as the orange butter on top will stop it forming a skin.

Meanwhile, preheat the oven to 220°C (425°F), Gas mark 7 (see tip below).

RACHEL'S TIP Turn the oven down to 200°C (400°F), Gas mark 6, at any stage during cooking if you think the top of the bread is golden enough and don't want it to burn. Some ovens cook more rapidly than others.

Bake the loaf in the oven for 20–25 minutes or until golden brown and crusty on top. At this stage you can take the loaf out of the oven, then carefully tip it out of the tin and return it to the oven for a further 10–15 minutes. When cooked it should sound hollow if tapped on the base. Remove from the oven and place on a wire rack to cool.

✳ To start preparing the bread in advance, you can mix cold instead of warm water with the yeast and leave the dough in the fridge to double in size. It will take 16–24 hours for the first rising (when the dough is in the bowl) and about 6 hours for the second rising/proving (when the dough has been cut and placed in the tin).

Though best eaten on the day, it will keep for up to three days in an airtight container. To serve, reheat it for a few minutes in a moderate oven (preheated to 180°C/350°F/Gas mark 4).

The orange butter can be made ahead and kept in the fridge for up to four days.

⊖ The quantities in this recipe are easy to double up if you'd like to make two loaves. Simply divide the dough in two after it has risen and roll out two separate rectangles before proceeding as above. You'll need two baking tins, of course, and don't forget to double the orange butter ingredients too.

PANCAKES WITH ORANGE BUTTER

One of the best ways of using orange butter (see page 226) is to serve it slathered over pancakes. It's a popular dessert we often make here at Ballymaloe Cookery School – not dissimilar to crêpes Suzette, though without the booze or the flambéing involved in the classic French dessert. You can either simply spread the butter over the freshly made pancakes or go a step further and reheat the cooked pancakes in a pan with the melted orange butter, as described below.

Makes 10–12 pancakes
25g (1oz) butter
1 quantity of orange butter (see the Orange
    Swirl Loaf on page 226)
Juice of 3 oranges (optional)

For the pancake batter
175g (6oz) plain flour
Pinch of salt
2 tsp caster sugar
3 eggs
Finely grated zest of 1 orange
200ml (7fl oz) milk

To make the pancake batter, sift the flour and salt into a mixing bowl and add the sugar. Make a well in the centre, then crack the eggs into it and add the orange zest. Pour the milk into the well, followed by 125ml (4½fl oz) of water, and using a whisk and stirring in rapid circles, mix everything together. The flour will gradually be incorporated into the liquid to form a batter. Continue to whisk until all lumps of flour have gone.

Once you're ready to cook the pancakes, place a frying pan (preferably non-stick or cast iron) on a high heat and allow it to get really hot. Place the butter on a plate and pour the batter into a jug. Have next to you a warmed plate (or a stack of individual plates) on which to tip the pancakes once they're cooked and a palette knife or fish slice for turning them over in the pan.

Dab a folded piece of kitchen paper into the butter to remove a piece about the size of a sugar cube. Carefully and quickly spread it over the inside of the hot pan, then pour over some of the batter. Swirl the pan as soon as the batter goes in. Try to pour in just enough to cover the base; if you do add too much, quickly pour the excess back into the jug. (If there's too much batter in the pan, the pancake will be too thick and stodgy.)

Allow the pancake to cook for 15–30 seconds (the time will depend on the level of heat and type of pan you are using, as well as the thickness of the pancake) or until golden underneath, then turn over with the help of the palette knife or fish slice and cook on the other side until golden. Flip or slide the pancake onto the plate (or one of the individual plates) – all the pancakes will sit happily on top of each other without the need for sheets of greaseproof paper in between.

Repeat the process for each pancake, buttering the pan every time, if necessary (it may not be if you're using a non-stick pan).

You can serve the pancakes straight away with a bowl of the orange butter. It needs to be soft enough to spread, so if it's been in the fridge take it out in advance to allow it to soften, and let everyone prepare their own by spreading about 2 teaspoons of butter over each pancake and rolling or folding it up to eat.

If you want to serve the pancakes in an orange sauce, then put the frying pan back on the hob, this time over a medium heat. Into the pan place a heaped dessertspoon of the orange butter and about 2 tablespoons of orange juice and allow the mixture to melt and get hot.

Place one cooked pancake in the pan, on top of the sauce, and tilt the pan slightly to allow some of the sauce to go over the top of the pancake. Once it's good and hot, fold the pancake in half and then in half again, then tip the pancake and all the sauce onto a warmed plate (for serving one person) or into a large serving dish (for serving everyone). Repeat with all the other pancakes.

If, after preparing all the pancakes, you have some orange butter and orange juice left over, then you can melt these together in the pan and pour them over the pancakes. These are completely divine served warm straight from the pan with cool, softly whipped cream or vanilla ice cream.

✳ If not being used straight away, the batter can be stored, covered, in the fridge for up to 24 hours.

The cooked pancakes in sauce will keep, covered in foil, in the oven (preheated to the lowest setting) for up to 30 minutes.

⊖⊕ You can halve or multiply the quantities in the recipe, depending on how big a crowd you are intending to feed.

WHITE CHOCOLATE AND RASPBERRY BREAD AND BUTTER PUDDING

The combination of white chocolate and raspberries is a real favourite of mine, one that's found its way into an assortment of different puddings down the years. Here, it works its magic once again to give a new take on this most classic of puddings. The dish is a great way of using up slightly stale bread, actually preferable to fresh in this recipe, being better at soaking up all that lovely sweet custard.

Serves 6–8
50g (2oz) butter, softened
12 slices of white bread, crusts removed
250g (9oz) fresh or frozen raspberries
200g (7oz) white chocolate, chopped into small pieces, or white chocolate chips
4 eggs
450ml (16fl oz) double or regular cream
225ml (8fl oz) milk
125g (4½oz) caster sugar
Pinch of salt
1 tbsp granulated sugar, for sprinkling

Equipment
20 x 25cm (8 x 10in) ovenproof dish

Butter the bread and arrange four slices, buttered side down, in a single layer in the dish. Scatter over half the raspberries and white chocolate pieces or chips, then cover with four more slices of bread, buttered side down again. Add the remaining raspberries and chocolate pieces/chips, followed by a final layer of bread, placed buttered side down (see tip below).

In a large bowl, whisk together the eggs with the cream, milk, caster sugar and salt. Pour this mixture over the bread through a fine sieve. Cover the dish with cling film and leave to stand for an hour, or in the fridge overnight.

When you're ready to bake the pudding, preheat the oven to 180°C (350°F), Gas mark 4.

Sprinkle the granulated sugar over the pudding, then prepare a bain-marie. Place the ovenproof dish in a large, deep-sided roasting tin and pour in enough boiling water to come about halfway up the sides of the pudding dish. This regulates the heat in the oven and ensures the eggs don't scramble.

Carefully transfer the dish and bain-marie to the oven and bake for about 1 hour or until the pudding is crisp and golden on top and just set in the centre – a skewer inserted into the middle will come out clean. Remove from the oven, allow to cool slightly and serve warm with cream or vanilla ice cream.

(✳) You could make this dish ahead up to the stage just before baking; it will keep in the fridge for up to 24 hours.

The pudding is at it's best warm, but I adore having cold bread and butter pudding in the fridge (where it will keep, covered, for a couple of days), if only to scoop up a quick spoonful when I'm hunting for something healthier!

(-+) You can easily halve the quantities in this recipe, using a dish of half the volume.

RACHEL'S TIP I sometimes cut each of the last four slices of bread into triangles (cutting each slice in half at an angle, then in half again) and arrange these, slightly overlapping, on the top of the pudding.

RUSTIC PLUM PIE

Fresh plums are a treat in the autumn; when just at their peak, they are incredibly sweet. That said, this recipe would also work well with other stone fruit, including peaches, nectarines or apricots. The pastry in this pie is particularly special, with an almost cake-like crumb that gives the finished dish a rustic touch that makes it a real favourite in our family. I like to serve it warm with a few scoops of vanilla ice cream.

Serves 6–8
75g (3oz) butter, cubed, plus 15g (½oz), softened, for greasing
250g (9oz) plain flour, plus extra for dusting
1 tsp baking powder
Pinch of salt
175g (6oz) caster sugar
1 egg
125ml (4½fl oz) milk
8 plums, stones removed and flesh quartered

Equipment
26cm (10¼in) diameter ovenproof pie plate

Preheat the oven to 180°C (350°F), Gas mark 4, and grease the pie plate with the 15g (½oz) softened butter.

Sift the flour, baking powder and salt into a large bowl, add 50g (2oz) of the sugar and mix well. Rub in the butter using your fingertips until the mixture resembles coarse breadcrumbs.

In a separate bowl, whisk the egg together with the milk. Make a well in the centre of the dry ingredients and pour in all but 2 tablespoons of the egg/milk liquid. Holding your fingers in a stiff claw shape, work you way round the bowl, mixing the wet ingredients into the dry ones until you have a soft dough (see tip below).

Divide the dough in half and dust one half with flour. (Keep the other half under a clean tea towel so that it doesn't dry out.) On a well-floured work surface, gently roll out this section of dough into a disc the size of the pie plate. Carefully transfer the pastry to the plate and pile the plums on top, leaving about 2cm (¾in) around the edge free. Scatter 100g (3½oz) of the remaining sugar over the plums.

Roll out the other half of the dough in the same way and place over the fruit to cover, pressing down around the edges. Brush the remaining egg/milk liquid over the dough, scatter with the rest of the sugar and bake in the oven for 40–50 minutes or until the fruit is soft when you test it with a skewer and the top of the pie is golden.

✱ The cooked pie will keep, covered, for up to two days. It's best served warm, so reheat in a moderate oven (preheated to 180°C/350°F/Gas mark 4).

RACHEL'S TIP The pastry for this pie should be like a scone dough, a bit wet, so don't handle it too much as any kind of kneading will toughen it. It should not look perfectly smooth, either, but comfortingly uneven and rustic. The minimum of handling is best; that way, you'll keep a lovely, tender crumbly crust.

NECTARINE AND STRAWBERRY FRANGIPANE

Frangipane is a divine combination of butter, almonds, sugar and eggs. It has long been used in tarts for its rich, buttery texture and gorgeous almond flavour. This recipe forgoes the tart shell for a simpler and purer dessert. The strawberries and nectarines, encased by the frangipane, stay sweet, tender and moist.

Serves 6–8
6 ripe nectarines (about 700g/1lb 9oz total
    weight), stones removed, and each fruit
    cut into eight wedges
300g (11oz) fresh strawberries, hulled
    and halved
Icing sugar, for dusting

For the frangipane
175g (6oz) butter, softened
250g (9oz) caster sugar
6 eggs
250g (9oz) ground almonds

Equipment
20 x 30cm (8 x 12in) ovenproof dish

Preheat the oven to 180°C (350°F), Gas mark 4.
    First make the frangipane. Place the butter
in a large bowl and beat until very soft. Add the
sugar and continue to mix until soft and light,
then beat in the eggs one by one. Finally, stir
in the ground almonds. Alternatively, place the
butter, sugar and eggs in a food processor and

whiz to combine, then add ground almonds
and whiz briefly until fully mixed in.
    Place the nectarines and strawberries in the
ovenproof dish, then spread the frangipane over
the top and bake in the oven (not too close to
the top or it may brown too quickly) for 40–50
minutes or until the frangipane is just set in the
centre. The nectarines by this stage should be
tender. Serve warm with a dusting of icing sugar
and a little softly whipped cream.

⊘ **Pear frangipane:** Replace the nectarines
and strawberries with 6 ripe pears, peeled,
cored and cut into roughly 2cm (¾in) chunks.

✳ The raw frangipane mixture can be made
ahead and stored, covered, in the fridge for
up to 12 hours.
    Once cooked, the frangipane will last
for up to two days if kept covered and stored
somewhere cool. While the dish is fine served
at room temperature, it's best reheated for a
few minutes in a moderate oven (preheated
to 180°C/350°F/Gas mark 4) to enjoy warm.

RASPBERRY UPSIDE-DOWN CAKE

**I make an upside-down cake at least every couple of weeks. I love the way the dish
starts off as a delicious dessert, ideal for rounding off a family meal. Then the next
day (if there's any left over!) it turns into the perfect coffee-time treat, to be enjoyed
in company or just on your own.**

Serves 6–8
50g (2oz) butter
125g (4½oz) caster sugar
250g (9oz) fresh or frozen raspberries

For the sponge
150g (5oz) butter, softened
150g (5oz) caster sugar
3 eggs
200g (7oz) self-raising flour, sifted

Equipment
25cm (10cm) diameter ovenproof frying pan
  (diameter measured at the top)

Preheat oven to 170°C (325°F), Gas mark 3.

Place the butter in the frying pan and melt
over a medium–high heat. Add the caster sugar,
stirring to mix, and cook for 1 minute. Remove
from the heat, then scatter the raspberries into
the pan so that they cover the base in a single
layer. Leave to sit while you make the sponge.

In a large bowl, beat the butter until soft, then
add the sugar and beat until pale and fluffy. Beat
in the eggs one at a time, then stir in the flour.
Alternatively, place all the ingredients in a food
processor and whiz together briefly until they
come together.

Spoon the sponge mixture over the raspberries
in blobs, then carefully spread it out to cover the
fruit in the pan.

Place in the oven and cook for 30–45 minutes
or until the sponge feels set in the centre – a skewer
inserted into the middle will come out clean. Allow
to sit for 2 minutes, then place a serving plate on
top of the pan and, clasping the plate firmly against
the pan, carefully flip it over. Lift off the pan to
reveal the pudding – now upside down on the plate,
with the raspberries on top. Serve warm or at room
temperature with perhaps a little cream.

✳ Any leftover cake will keep (covered with a
cake cover or an upturned bowl so as not to squash
the raspberries) for up to two days.

PEACHES WITH MASCARPONE, PISTACHIOS AND HONEY

This dish is like an exotic peaches and cream but using mascarpone instead. And the effect is just divine, the tangy cheese offset by the juicy peaches, sweet honey and crunchy pistachios. A great example of how something totally simple can be hugely impressive.

Serves 5
Butter, for greasing
5 fresh peaches
3 tbsp mascarpone
3 tbsp runny honey, plus extra for drizzling
50g (2oz) shelled pistachios, roughly chopped

Preheat the oven to 200°C (400°F), Gas mark 6, and grease a medium-sized ovenproof dish with a little butter.

If you prefer the peaches to be skinless, cut a cross in the bottom of each peach, cutting through the skin, and place in a heatproof bowl. Pour over enough freshly boiled water to cover and leave for 1 minute. Carefully remove the peaches from the bowl using a slotted spoon and peel off the skins. Cut each peach in half, removing the stone, and place, cut side up, in the ovenproof dish. Cover with foil and bake in the oven for 20–25 minutes or until peaches are soft.

While the peaches are cooking, mix together the mascarpone and honey in a bowl.

Tip the pistachios into a non-stick frying pan and toast over a high heat for a minute or two, tossing regularly to avoid burning. Take off the heat and set aside to cool.

Remove the peaches from the oven and spoon the mascarpone and honey mixture into the cavity of each peach half, dividing the mixture equally between the fruit. Serve the peaches with a little extra honey drizzled over the mascarpone and the toasted pistachios scattered on top.

⊝ Simply double the quantities in the recipe to serve 10.

BUTTERSCOTCH APPLE PUDDING

A firm family favourite in our house, this delicious pudding is fast to whip up and results in two layers: a base of soft juicy apples sitting in a butterscotch sauce and topped by a delicious toffee sponge.

Serves 4–6

2 large cooking apples (about 450g/1lb total weight), peeled, cored and cut into roughly 2cm (¾in) dice
125g (4½oz) self-raising flour
¼ tsp salt
200g (7oz) brown sugar, plus 2 tbsp for sprinkling
100g (3½oz) butter, melted
1 tsp vanilla extract
1 egg
200ml (7fl oz) milk
2 tbsp golden syrup
150ml (5fl oz) boiling water

Equipment
20 x 30cm (8 x 12in) ovenproof dish

Preheat the oven to 180°C (350°F), Gas mark 4.

Place the apple pieces in the bottom of the ovenproof dish, spreading them out to form an even layer.

Sift the flour and salt into a large bowl and mix in half the sugar. In another bowl, mix together the melted butter, vanilla extract, egg and milk.

Pour the wet ingredients into the dry ones, then whisk briefly to bring everything together. Pour the mixture into the dish, distributing it evenly over the apples.

Next, place the golden syrup in a saucepan with the boiling water and remaining sugar. Bring to the boil, stirring to dissolve the sugar, then pour this evenly over the mixture in the dish. Most of it will sink through the pudding mixture to the bottom of the dish, but don't be alarmed – this creates a beautiful butterscotch sauce underneath the sponge when baked.

To finish, sprinkle over the 2 tablespoons of brown sugar, then place in the oven and bake for about 30 minutes or until the top of the pudding has a very light spring when you press it with your finger. This is best served warm with softly whipped cream or vanilla ice cream.

✳ Any leftover pudding will keep well in the fridge for up to three days; simply reheat in a moderate oven (preheated to 180°C/350°F/Gas mark 4) for just a few minutes to warm through.

CHOCOLATE MOUSSE WITH SALTED CARAMEL SAUCE AND SHORTBREAD BISCUITS

✳ ⊖

A chocolate mousse is one of the easiest desserts to make but no less impressive because of it. The intense chocolate flavour is often enough as it is, but I like to enhance it with orange zest or brandy. You could serve the mousse on its own, with cream or, for a true celebration of flavour, with this salted caramel sauce and shortbread biscuits.

CHOCOLATE MOUSSE

Serves 4–6
120ml (4fl oz) double or regular cream
120g (4oz) dark chocolate (55–70% cocoa solids),
    broken into pieces, or dark chocolate drops
½–1 tsp finely grated orange zest, or 2 tbsp
    orange liqueur or brandy
2 eggs, separated

Bring the cream to the boil in a saucepan, remove from the heat, add the chocolate to the cream and stir until the chocolate melts. Add the orange zest or liqueur/brandy and whisk in the egg yolks.

In a separate, clean, dry bowl, whisk the egg whites until just stiff, then stir a quarter of the egg whites into the cream mixture. Gently fold in the rest of the whites, then spoon into little bowls, glasses or cups and leave for 2 hours in the fridge to set. Serve with the salted caramel sauce and shortbread biscuits (see following recipes).

✳ The mousse will keep, covered, in the fridge for up to two days.

SALTED CARAMEL SAUCE

Makes about 375ml (13fl oz)
225g (8oz) caster or granulated sugar
110g (4oz) butter
175ml (6fl oz) double or regular cream
Good pinch of salt (see tip opposite)

Place the sugar in a saucepan with 75ml (3fl oz) of water and set on a medium heat, stirring the syrup as it heats up to dissolve the sugar. Once the sugar has dissolved, stir in the butter, then turn the heat up and cook for 10 minutes or until the mixture turns a toffee colour. Do not stir it as it cooks, but do swirl the pan occasionally if the caramel is turning golden on one side of the pan before the other.

Once the caramel is a rich golden toffee colour, take it off the heat and stir in half the cream. When the bubbles die down, stir in the rest of the cream and salt to taste. Serve with the chocolate mousse and shortbread biscuits.

✳ This sauce can be made ahead and stored in the fridge for about three weeks. Simply reheat in a pan on the hob when you're ready to serve.

⊖ The quantities double up perfectly. In fact, they quadruple perfectly too. You can never have too much salted caramel sauce in the fridge, in my view! It's great drizzled over vanilla ice cream.

Makes 15–25 biscuits

150g (5oz) plain flour, sifted, plus extra
  for dusting
50g (2oz) caster sugar
100g (3½oz) butter, softened

Preheat the oven to 180°C (350°F), Gas mark 4.

Mix the flour and sugar together in a large bowl. Rub in the butter, bringing the mixture together to form a stiff dough (don't be tempted to add any water). Alternatively, bring together the ingredients in a food processor. Transfer the dough to a work surface lightly dusted in flour and roll it out to a thickness of about 5mm (¼in). Cut into shapes – fingers, rounds or whatever you like – and place on two baking sheets, spaced evenly apart. Bake for 6–10 minutes or until pale golden in colour.

Remove from the oven and, using a palette knife or metal fish slice, carefully transfer the biscuits to a wire rack to cool. Serve with the chocolate mousse and salted caramel sauce.

✳ You could make the shortbread in advance as it will keep in an airtight container for up to four days.

RACHEL'S TIP How much salt you use in the caramel sauce will depend on personal preference, and the type of salt. I love salt flakes such as Maldon or Atlantic sea salt.

QUICK DOUBLE CHOCOLATE MILLIONAIRE'S SHORTBREAD

✳

This is a fast version of classic millionaire's shortbread (sometimes called Wellington squares) in which the toffee layer is made from scratch. The shortcut here involves using dulce de leche (a sweet, thick milky caramel originating in South America) or ready-boiled tins of condensed milk. How to boil your own tins of condensed milk is explained in the tip below. Do make sure, however, to buy full-fat condensed milk; the version labelled 'light' will not work.

Makes 20 large rectangles or 40 small squares or triangles
2 x 397g tins of dulce de leche (also labelled 'caramel'), or 2 x 397g tins of full-fat condensed milk, boiled (see tip below)
300g (11oz) dark chocolate (55–70% cocoa solids) or milk chocolate, broken into pieces, or dark or milk chocolate drops/chips
75g (3oz) white chocolate, broken into pieces, or white chocolate drops/chips

For the shortbread biscuit base
200g (7oz) butter, plus extra for greasing
300g (3½oz) plain flour, sifted
100g (3½oz) caster sugar

Equipment
25 x 40cm (10 x 16in) baking tin or Swiss roll tin

Preheat the oven to 180°C (350°F), Gas mark 4, and grease the baking tin (or Swiss roll tin) with butter.

First make the shortbread biscuit base. Mix together the flour and sugar in a bowl, then rub in the butter with your fingertips so that the mixture resembles fine breadcrumbs. Tip the mixture into the greased tin and press down with your hands to ensure the surface is even.

Place in the oven and bake for 20 minutes or until light golden all over, then remove from the oven and allow to cool on a wire rack, leaving the shortbread in the tin.

Pour the dulce de leche or boiled condensed milk over the shortbread once it has cooled, and smooth over evenly with a palette knife or spatula. Place in the fridge to chill for 20 minutes.

Meanwhile, place the dark or milk chocolate pieces in a heatproof bowl and the white chocolate in another bowl. Set each bowl over a saucepan of simmering water and allow the chocolate to melt.

Remove the caramel-covered shortbread from the fridge and pour over the melted dark or milk chocolate, smoothing it out evenly using a palette knife or spatula. Swirl over the white chocolate, then leave to set in a cool part of your kitchen but not the fridge. Cut into squares, rectangles or triangles to serve.

✳ Stored in an airtight container, these will keep for about five days.

RACHEL'S TIP If using condensed milk, place the unopened tins in a large saucepan, cover with plenty of cold water and bring to the boil. Leave to boil for 2½ hours, topping up the water from time to time to ensure there is still plenty in the pan. Remove from the heat and leave the tins to cool down completely in the water.

PEANUT BUTTER SHORTBREAD BISCUITS

Americans just adore peanut butter and they love adding it to everything, especially if it's sweet. Indeed, there are few sweet recipes that they haven't tried adding it to at some point – for good reason, as the salty-sweet combination is irresistible. These biscuits are no exception. You can enjoy them on their own, of course, but they are also wonderful served with various desserts, such as with the chocolate mousse and salted caramel sauce (see page 242) instead of the plain shortbread biscuits, or with vanilla ice cream and the same sauce.

Makes 20 biscuits
300g (11oz) plain flour, sifted, plus extra
   for dusting
200g (7oz) soft light brown sugar
200g (7oz) crunchy peanut butter
150g (5oz) butter, softened
1 tsp vanilla extract
Demerara sugar, for sprinkling

Equipment
6cm (2½in) diameter pastry cutter

Preheat the oven to 180°C (350°F), Gas mark 4, and line two baking sheets with baking parchment.

Place all the ingredients, apart from the demerara sugar, into a large bowl. Rub together with your fingertips until the mixture resembles coarse breadcrumbs, then bring the crumbs together to form a soft dough. Alternatively, place the ingredients in a food processor and mix briefly to combine.

Transfer the dough to your worktop, using a little flour to dust the work surface and the top of the dough to prevent it from sticking. Roll out the dough to a thickness of about 5mm (¼in) thick and cut into rounds with the pastry cutter.

Use a fork to prick each biscuit a couple of times, then place on the prepared baking sheets and bake for about 8–12 minutes or until light golden in colour. (Unless you have a fan oven, you will need to bake the biscuits in two batches.) Take out of the oven and, while the biscuits are still warm, sprinkle with the demerara sugar. Carefully remove from the trays using a palette knife or metal fish slice and place on a wire rack to cool.

✳ The dough will keep in the fridge for up to two weeks. If you roll it, or any dough that's left over, into a sausage about 6cm (2½in) in diameter (or 4cm/1½in for smaller biscuits), you can simply cut a few biscuits at a time as you need them. Just keep the dough in the fridge wrapped in baking parchment or cling film, then whenever you want some biscuits you can cut a few slices, about 5mm (¼in) thick, and cook as above.

The dough can also be kept in the freezer (for up to three months), either in one piece or cut into biscuits. The uncooked biscuits can be baked from frozen, although they will require a few minutes' extra cooking time.

The cooked biscuits can be stored in the freezer, where they will keep for up to three months.

⊖ Double the quantities to make 40 biscuits.

DOUBLE CHOCOLATE CHIP COOKIES

Crisp, chewy, buttery and unashamedly chocolatey – when cookies are this good, it makes me think they're the reason ovens were invented. If you are a confirmed chocoholic (and I most certainly am), then why have a single dose when you can have double?

Makes 20 large cookies

225g (8oz) butter, softened
325g (11½oz) caster sugar
2 eggs
1 tsp vanilla extract
225g (8oz) plain flour
75g (3oz) cocoa powder
1 tsp bicarbonate of soda
¼ tsp salt
175g (6oz) dark chocolate (55–70% cocoa solids), chopped into small pieces, or dark chocolate chips

Preheat the oven to 180°C (350°F), Gas mark 4. Line three baking sheets with baking parchment.

Place the butter in a large bowl and beat until very soft. Add the sugar and beat until the mixture is pale and fluffy. Crack in one egg at a time, beating between each addition, then add the vanilla extract. Sift in the flour, cocoa powder, bicarbonate of soda and salt, then add the chocolate pieces/chips and fold in to combine. Alternatively, place all the ingredients except the chocolate pieces/chips in a food processor and whiz briefly until they come together, then fold in the chocolate.

With wet hands, form the dough into balls each the size of a golf ball (or use two soup spoons to scoop up and shape the same amount of dough). Arrange on the prepared baking sheets, placing 6–7 balls of dough on each sheet and leaving space for the cookies to spread.

Bake for 10–14 minutes or until the cookies look slightly cracked on top. (With three baking sheets, you will need to cook them in three batches, or two batches in a fan oven.) Take out of the oven and allow to cool for a few minutes, then remove from the baking sheets using a palette knife or metal fish slice and place on a wire rack to cool down completely.

✳ The dough will keep in the fridge for up to three weeks. I like to roll it into a log/sausage then store it, covered in baking parchment or cling film, in the fridge. Whenever you fancy a few cookies, you can simply cut off slices about 5mm (¼in) thick and bake them as above, reducing the cooking time slightly.

The cookies will keep in an airtight container for up to four days.

⊖ Double the quantities in the recipe to make 40 cookies, or halve the amount if you'd like to make only 10 (though you can never have enough, believe me!).

CHOCOLATE COOKIES AND CREAM CHEESECAKE

There is nothing subtle about this seriously indulgent mascarpone cheesecake. Not for the faint-hearted, it is full on yet makes for a magnificent (if rare) treat. Any chocolate biscuits will do, although I particularly like using Double Chocolate Chip Cookies (see page 249).

Serves 8–10

15g (½oz) cocoa powder, sifted
25ml (1fl oz) strong coffee, such as espresso
1 tsp vanilla extract
500g (1lb 2oz) mascarpone
400ml (14fl oz) double or regular cream
50g (2oz) icing sugar
9–12 chocolate cookies or chocolate chip cookies
50g (2oz) dark chocolate (55–75% cocoa solids), grated, for sprinkling

Equipment

23cm (9in) diameter spring-form cake tin
   (see tip below)

In a large bowl, whisk together the cocoa powder, coffee, vanilla extract, mascarpone, cream and icing sugar for 1–2 minutes or until thick.

Arrange one-third (3–4) of the cookies (whole) in the bottom of the cake tin, then spread over one-third of the chocolate cream mixture. Add a second layer of cookies, then another layer of chocolate cream, followed by the remaining cookies and a final layer of chocolate cream.

Use a spatula to smooth the top layer of chocolate cream, then cover the tin with cling film and place in the fridge to chill for eight hours or overnight.

To remove the cheesecake from the cake tin, run a small, sharp knife around the cheesecake to loosen the edges, then unfasten the clip and lift away the sides of the tin. Using a palette knife or a metal fish slice, loosen the cheesecake from the base of the tin and carefully slide off onto a plate. Sprinkle with the grated chocolate to serve.

✳ The cheesecake will keep, covered, for up to 48 hours in the fridge.

RACHEL'S TIP It's much easier to remove the finished cheesecake from the cake tin if you turn the base of the tin over, so that the 'lip' is facing down, before placing it in the tin and filling with the cheesecake mixture.

SWEDISH CARDAMOM COOKIES

✳ ⊖

I first tasted these divine butter cookies in Sweden about six years ago, served with a strong cup of coffee. Each one had an outer rim of crunchy coloured sugar, although chopped pecans would work equally well – as I've suggested here.

Makes about 40 cookies

225g (8oz) butter, softened
125g (4½oz) icing sugar
275g (10oz) plain flour, sifted, plus extra
  for dusting
1 egg, beaten
2 tsp ground cardamom (see tip below)
1 tsp finely grated orange zest
Pinch of salt
200g (7oz) chopped pecans or sugar crystals
  (also known as sugar nibs, available in different
  colours from speciality shops) (optional)

Place the butter in a bowl and beat until soft. Add half the icing sugar and continue to beat, then add the other half and keep beating until the sugar is fully incorporated. Next add the flour, egg, cardamom, orange zest and salt, and continue to beat until well combined. Alternatively, place all the ingredients in a food processor and whiz briefly to combine.

On a worktop lightly dusted in flour, roll the dough into a log shape approximately 4cm (1½in) in diameter and 35cm (14in) long. Sprinkle the chopped pecans or sugar crystals (if using) onto a large piece of baking parchment or cling film, then roll the dough log in the nuts/ sugar crystals to coat before rolling up the dough in the paper/cling film. If not adding the nuts/

sugar, then simply roll up the dough log in the paper/cling film.

Place the wrapped dough in the fridge to chill for a few hours or overnight.

When you are ready to cook the cookies, preheat the oven to 180°C (350°F), Gas mark 4, and line two baking sheets with baking parchment.

Remove the dough from the fridge and cut into slices 5–7mm (⅛–¼in) thick. Transfer the slices to the prepared baking sheets and bake in the oven for 15–20 minutes (the time varying according to the thickness of the cookies) or until light golden. (Unless you have a fan oven, you will need to bake the cookies in two batches.) Using a palette knife or metal fish slice, carefully lift onto a wire rack to cool.

✳ Once rolled into a log, the dough can be kept in the fridge and cut into slices for cooking as and when you need them. Wrapped in baking parchment or cling film, the dough will keep for up to two weeks; it will also keep in the freezer for up to three months.

Though best eaten fresh, the cookies will keep in an airtight container for up to three days.

⊖ You can double the quantities in this recipe if you'd like more cookies. It's worth making two logs, in fact, as you can always keep one in the freezer.

RACHEL'S TIP   Use freshly ground seeds from green cardamom pods, if at all possible, for the best flavour. Crush the pods with the end of a rolling pin and grind the seeds using a pestle and mortar or place in a plastic bag and use the rolling pin to crush them.

APPLE CUSTARD TART

This is very similar to a classic French Besançon apple tart. Other seasonal fruit work beautifully, too: try peaches, apricots, rhubarb and gooseberries, though leave out the cinnamon and use vanilla extract instead.

Serves 6

For the tart case
200g (7oz) plain flour
1 tbsp icing sugar
Pinch of salt
100g (3½oz) chilled butter, diced
½–1 egg, beaten

For the filling
250ml (9fl oz) double or regular cream
100g (3½oz) caster sugar
3 eggs
½ tsp ground cinnamon
2–3 eating apples, cored, peeled and thinly sliced

For the apricot glaze
5 tbsp apricot jam
Juice of ½ lemon

Equipment
23cm (9in) diameter, fluted, loose-bottomed tart tin with 2cm (¾in) sides

First make the tart case. Sift the flour, sugar and salt into a bowl and rub in the butter until the mixture resembles coarse breadcrumbs. Add half the beaten egg and, using your hands, bring the dough together, adding a little more egg if it is too dry to come together.

If you are making the pastry in a food processor, sift in the flour, sugar and salt and add the butter. Whiz for a few seconds, then add half the beaten egg and whiz for just a few more seconds until it comes together. You might need to add a little more egg, but don't add too much – it should just come together. Don't over-process the pastry or it will be tough and heavy. Reserve the remaining beaten egg for brushing over the finished pastry.

Without kneading the dough, carefully shape it into a round, 1–2cm (½–¾in) thick, using your hands to flatten it. Cover with cling film and place in the fridge to chill for about 30 minutes.

Preheat the oven to 180°C (350°F), Gas mark 4.

Take the pastry out of the fridge and place it between two sheets of cling film (each bigger than your tart tin). Using a rolling pin, roll out the pastry to about 3mm (⅛in) thick. Make sure to keep it in a round shape and large enough to line the base and sides of the tin.

Removing just the top layer of cling film, place the pastry upside down (cling-film side facing up) in the tart tin. (There's no need to flour or grease the tin.) Press the pastry into the edges of the tin, with the cling film still attached to the dough, and using your thumb 'cut' the pastry along the edge of the tin for a neat finish. If there are any holes or gaps in the pastry, simply patch them up with some of your spare pieces of dough.

Remove the cling film and chill the pastry in the fridge for 15 minutes or the freezer for 5 minutes.

Remove the pastry from the fridge or freezer and line with greaseproof paper or baking parchment, leaving plenty of paper to come up the sides. Fill the lined tart case with baking beans or dried pulses and bake 'blind' for 20–25 minutes or until the pastry feels just dry to the touch on the base.

Remove the paper and beans, brush with a little of the remaining beaten egg and return to the oven for 3 minutes. Again, if there are any little holes or cracks in the pastry, patch them up with leftover dough before returning to the oven. Once the pastry has been baked blind, take it out of the oven (leaving it switched on) and set aside in the tin while you make the filling.

In a bowl, whisk together the cream, sugar, eggs and cinnamon until thoroughly mixed.

Place the apple slices in the pastry case, starting at the edge and arranging the slices so that they fan out in concentric circles. Slowly pour the custard mixture over the apples through a sieve.

Carefully place the filled tart in the oven, and bake for 30–40 minutes or until the custard is golden and just set in the centre. Take out of the oven and leave to cool, still in the tin, for 5 minutes.

Meanwhile, heat the apricot jam and lemon juice in a small saucepan on a medium heat. Stir constantly until it's quite runny. Pour through a clean sieve and, while the glaze is hot, carefully brush over the tart, covering all the filling. Allow the tart to cool down, then take out of the tin and transfer to a plate to serve.

⊘ **Apricot custard tart:** Replace the apples with 8–10 fresh apricots, stones removed and apricots halved, and arrange cut side down in the tart case.
Rhubarb custard tart: Replace the apples with 175g (6oz) of rhubarb, trimmed and sliced into 2cm (¾in) lengths. (Halve big stalks lengthways first.)

✳ The dough can be chilled, wrapped in cling film, for up to 24 hours, or frozen for up to three months.

The uncooked tart case will keep for several weeks in the freezer (well wrapped in foil or cling film). Equally, it can be baked a day in advance and kept covered until you fill it.

The filled, cooked tart will keep – covered with an upturned bowl – for up to three days.

FRENCH TOAST WITH CINNAMON MASCARPONE

French toast is an excellent way of using up any leftover stale bread, as reflected in the French name for the dish, pain perdu or 'lost bread'. Try making it for an uncompromisingly luxurious breakfast – a wonderfully wicked way to start a lazy Sunday.

Serves 4
4 eggs
2 tbsp double or regular cream
½ tsp ground cinnamon
½ tsp vanilla extract
Pinch of salt
25g (1oz) butter
4 slices of white bread

For the cinnamon mascarpone
150g (5oz) mascarpone
1 tbsp maple syrup
½ tsp ground cinnamon

To serve
Icing sugar
Maple syrup

First make the cinnamon mascarpone. In a bowl, whisk together the mascarpone, maple syrup and cinnamon until combined. Cover with cling film and leave in the fridge while you make the French toast.

In a separate bowl, whisk the eggs together with the cream, cinnamon, vanilla and salt.

Set a frying pan over a medium heat and add half the butter. When the butter has melted and is foaming, dip two slices of bread in the egg mixture, making sure each piece is completely covered, then carefully place them in the frying pan. Fry for 2–3 minutes on each side or until golden brown. Place on separate plates, then melt the remaining butter, dip the last two slices of bread in the egg mixture and fry in the same way.

Dust the French toast with icing sugar, drizzle with plenty of maple syrup and serve with the cinnamon mascarpone and perhaps some sliced apple and banana.

✳ French toast is best eaten as soon as it's made, though the cinnamon mascarpone could be made ahead and stored in the fridge, covered, for up to three days.

⊖⊕ You can halve or double up the quantities in the recipe, if you like. If doubling, you may want to use more than one frying pan so all the toast is ready at the same time.

MERINGUES

The perfect way to round off a leisurely Sunday lunch, meringues satisfy that craving for sweetness without being too filling. Adding some whipped cream and fresh berries (see serving suggestions below) are all you need for a feast of contrasting texture and flavour. Making meringues is also an excellent way of using up leftover egg whites (see tip below).

Makes 10–15 meringues
4 egg whites
Pinch of salt
300g (11oz) caster sugar
1 tsp vanilla extract

Equipment
Piping bag fitted with a ½–1cm (¼–½in) nozzle
  (optional)

Preheat the oven to 140°C (275°F), Gas mark 1, and line two baking sheets with baking parchment.

Place the egg whites in a large, spotlessly clean bowl, add the salt and whisk into soft peaks. Add the sugar, 1 tablespoon at a time, whisking between each addition. Continue whisking until all the sugar has been added and the meringue forms stiff, glossy peaks.

Using a large spatula or metal spoon, fold in the vanilla extract. With a tablespoon or dessert-spoon, scoop up a heaped spoonful of the meringue mixture, then use a second spoon to scrape the mixture onto one of the lined baking sheets. Repeat with the remaining mixture, leaving a little room in between each meringue.

Alternatively, spoon the meringue mixture into the piping bag and pipe a series of small mounds or rosettes, each approximately 7cm (2¾in) in diameter, onto the prepared baking sheets.

Bake in the oven for about 30 minutes. (Unless you have a fan oven, you will need to bake the meringues in two batches.) To test whether the meringues are ready, gently lift up one and press the base – it should be crisp but give way with a bit of pressure. If possible, allow to cool down completely in the oven, with the heat switched off and the door slightly ajar. Transfer the cooked meringues to a wire rack – they will crisp up further as they cool.

Serving suggestions
The meringues could be served sandwiched together with whipped cream and raspberries. For this many meringues you would need 375g (13oz) of fresh raspberries and 250ml (9fl oz) of double or regular cream that has been softly whipped. You could also use the Summer Fruit Compote (see page 222) instead of fresh rasp-berries. I also like serving meringues with sliced bananas and salted caramel sauce (see page 242).

✳ Once made, the meringues will keep in an airtight tin for up to four weeks.

📦 Use any broken meringues for making Eton mess or the Iced Strawberry Meringue Cake (see page 258).

RACHEL'S TIP Egg whites can be stored in a jar in the fridge for up to two weeks. Each weighs approximately 30g (1¼oz), or 30ml (1¼fl oz) in volume, making it easy to measure out the right amount of egg white for a specific recipe.

ICED STRAWBERRY MERINGUE CAKE

**When I was younger, my mum used to make a dessert very similar to this and I've always
loved it. The beauty of this dish is that it can be made using up leftover meringues,
although I often make meringues especially for it too. It would be equally delicious made
with raspberries – see ⊘ below for other ideas that you might like to try.**

Serves 8–10
500ml (18fl oz) double or regular cream
265g (9½oz) meringues (see ✳ below),
   broken into roughly 2cm (¾in) chunks

For the strawberry sauce
200g (7oz) fresh strawberries, hulled
   and quartered
Juice of 1 lemon
50g (2oz) icing sugar

Equipment
23cm (9in) diameter spring-form cake tin

Line the cake tin with a double layer of cling film
and then make the strawberry sauce. In a food
processor or blender, whiz the strawberries with
the lemon juice and icing sugar, then pour the
mixture through a sieve into a bowl and discard
the seeds left in the sieve.

Pour the cream into another bowl and whisk
into soft peaks, then crumble the meringue into
the whipped cream and stir together to mix.
Add the strawberry sauce, swirling it through
the cream and meringue mixture.

Tip the mixture into the lined cake tin and
smooth the surface with a spatula. Wrap the tin

in cling film and freeze for at least eight hours
or preferably overnight.

Take the frozen cake from the freezer, then
unclip the sides of the tin and carefully lift these
away. Remove the cling film from the sides of the
cake, then use a palette knife or metal fish slice
to carefully transfer the cake from the base of
the tin to a serving plate. Cut into slices to serve,
either on its own or with fresh strawberries.

⊘ **Iced raspberry meringue cake:** Replace the
strawberries with the same quantity of fresh or
frozen and defrosted raspberries.
Iced lemon meringue cake: Replace the
strawberry sauce with 200g (7oz) lemon curd.
Iced toffee meringue cake: Try using 200g (7oz)
dulce de leche (see page 245) instead of the
strawberry sauce.

✳ You could make up the meringues on page
257 for this dish or use any leftover broken
pieces. Any leftover pavlova would work well too.

The strawberry sauce could be made ahead
and kept in the fridge for up to three days.

The cake will keep in the freezer, well covered,
for up to two months.

CONVERSION CHARTS

DRY WEIGHTS

GRAMS (g)	OUNCES (OZ)	GRAMS (g)	OUNCES (OZ)
5	¼	500	1lb 2oz
8/10	⅓	550	1lb 3oz
15	½	600g	1lb 5oz
20	¾	625g	1lb 6oz
25	1	650	1lb 7oz
30/35	1¼	675	1½lb
40	1½	700	1lb 9oz
50	2	750	1lb 10oz
60/70	2½	800	1¾lb
75/85/90	3	850	1lb 14oz
100	3½	900	2lb
110/120	4	950	2lb 2oz
125/130	4½	1kg	2lb 3oz
135/140/150	5	1.1kg	2lb 6oz
170/175	6	1.25kg	2¾lb
200	7	1.3/1.4kg	3lb
225	8	1.5kg	3lb 5oz
250	9	1.75/1.8kg	4lb
265	9½	2kg	4lb 4oz
275	10	2.25kg	5lb
300	11	2.5kg	5½lb
325	11½	3kg	6½lb
350	12	3.5kg	7¾lb
375	13	4kg	8¾lb
400	14	4.5kg	9¾lb
425	15	6.8kg	15lb
450	1lb	9kg	20lb
475	1lb 1oz		

568ml = 1 UK pint (20fl oz)
16fl oz = 1 US pint

LIQUID MEASURES

METRIC (ml)	IMPERIAL (fl oz)	CUPS
15	½	1 tbsp (level)
20	¾	
25	1	⅛
30	1¼	
50	2	¼
60	2½	
75	3	
100	3½	⅜
110/120	4	½
125	4½	
150	5	⅔
175	6	¾
200/215	7	
225	8	1
250	9	
275	9½	
300	½ pint	1¼
350	12	1½
375	13	
400	14	

METRIC (ml)	IMPERIAL (fl oz)	CUPS
425	15	
450	16	2
500	18	2¼
550	19	
600	1 pint	2½
700	1¼ pints	
750	1⅓ pints	
800	1 pint 9 fl oz	
850	1½ pints	
900	1 pint 12 fl oz	3¾
1 litre	1¾ pints	1 quart (4 cups)
1.2 litres	2 pints	1¼ quarts
1.25 litres	2¼ pints	
1.5 litres	2½ pints	3 US pints
1.75/1.8 litres	3 pints	
2 litres	3½ pints	2 quarts
2.2 litres	3¾ pints	
2.5 litres	4⅓ pints	
3 litres	5 pints	
3.5 litres	6 pints	

OVEN TEMPERATURES

°C	°F	GAS MARK	DESCRIPTION
110	225	¼	cool
130	250	½	cool
140	275	1	very low
150	300	2	very low
160/170	325	3	low to moderate
180	350	4	moderate
190	375	5	moderately hot
200	400	6	hot
220	425	7	hot
230	450	8	hot
240	475	9	very hot

INDEX

red cabbage: honey-roasted duck with red cabbage 104–5
  pork sliders with red cabbage salad 163
red lentil soup with cumin and coriander 194
refried black bean fajitas 139
refried black beans 138–9
rhubarb custard tart 255
rice: easy arancini with crème fraîche herb sauce 53
  minestrone 174–5
  pilaf rice 190
  saffron rice with sultanas and pistachios 190
  smoked salmon and lemon risotto with asparagus 50
  Spanish chicken 102
risotto: easy arancini with crème fraîche herb sauce 53
  smoked salmon and lemon risotto with asparagus 50
rolls: pork sliders with red cabbage salad 163
  pulled lamb toasted baps 150
  white yeast rolls 43
root vegetable gratin 219
rosemary: caramelised onion and rosemary bread 46–7
  rosemary and garlic spatchcock chicken with bulgur wheat salad 90–1
  slow-roast pork belly with rosemary 160
rustic plum pie 233

S

saffron: saffron clams 73
  saffron rice with sultanas and pistachios 190
salads: broccoli orzo salad 204
  bulgur wheat salad 90–1
  chicken, fennel and orange salad 98–9
  nutty quinoa salad 185
  panzanella 203

pickled beetroot, sweet potato and lentil salad 193
  pork sliders with red cabbage salad 163
  roasted butternut squash salad 216
  watercress and orange salad 100–1
salami: broccoli orzo salad 204
salmon: potato, smoked salmon and dill tart 50–1
  smoked salmon and lemon risotto with asparagus 50
salsa, tomato 74
salted caramel sauce 242–3
sandwiches: pork sliders with red cabbage salad 163
  pulled lamb toasted baps 150
satay, pork 168
sauces: cheese sauce 133
  crème fraîche sauce 53
  gravy 160
  lemon aioli 150
  lemon and herb aioli 92–3
  Mornay sauce 66–7
  pesto 31
  plum sauce 112
  ragù 133
  salted caramel sauce 242–3
  spicy peanut sauce 168
  tapenade 31
  tomato sauce 128–9
sausages: sausage pasta pot 167
  see also chorizo
sesame seeds: sesame pak choi 198
  toasting 198
shallots: roast chicken pieces with lemon and herb aioli 92–3
shellfish see mussels, prawns etc.
shepherd's pie 154
sherry: chicken livers with sherry 95
  saffron clams 73
shortbread: peanut butter shortbread biscuits 246
  quick double chocolate millionaire's shortbread 245

shortbread biscuits 242–3
shortcrust pastry 50
shrimps see prawns
skewers: meatball skewers 137
  pork satay with spicy peanut sauce 168
smoked haddock: instant cullen skink 64
  smoked haddock pie 63
smoked mackerel tart 58
smoked salmon: potato, smoked salmon and dill tart 50–1
  smoked salmon and lemon risotto with asparagus 50
soups: Chinese-style duck soup 108
  instant cullen skink 64
  lamb and pearl barley broth 153
  minestrone 174–5
  prawn bisque with garlic mayonnaise croûtons 77
  red lentil soup with cumin and coriander 194
  Thai butternut squash soup 215
  Thai pork noodle soup 178–9
sour cream: lime chive cream 134–5
soy sauce: duck breasts with plum sauce and vegetable stir-fry 112
spaghetti: cheesy meatballs with spaghetti 128–9
  prawn and asparagus spaghetti 78
Spanish chicken 102
spiced lamb gigot chops 157
spices, toasting 27, 36
spicy spatchcock chicken with watercress and orange salad 100–1
spinach: Moroccan chickpea tagine 182–3
  spinach, bacon and Gruyère frittata 116
  spinach, potato and Gruyère frittata 116
  spinach, red pepper and Gruyère frittata 116
spring onions: duck breasts with plum sauce and vegetable stir-fry 112

ACKNOWLEDGEMENTS

A great big cheer for, and huge heartfelt thanks to, each and every person involved in the creation of this book. At Collins: Helen Wedgewood, Laura Nickoll, Martin Topping and Carole Tonkinson. Louise Evans and Peter Dawson at Grade Design. Tara Fisher who took all the beautiful shots, Joss Herd who cooked for and styled all the beautiful shots, Liz Belton, Kate Parker, Diarmaid Falvey, Josh Heller, Sam Head, Victoria Grier, Elaine Hayes and Sinead Doran.

Thanks so much to Fiona, Alison, Maclean Lindsay and Roz Ellman at Limelight Management. And a great big hug to Lucy Downes of Sphere One for the divine Irish cashmere.

Thanks also to everyone at Ballymaloe House and Cookery School, and to all my amazing family and friends for the never-ending support. And last but certainly not least, my husband Isaac to whom I dedicate this book.

HarperCollins*Publishers*
77–85 Fulham Palace Road
London W6 8JB
www.harpercollins.co.uk

First published by HarperCollins*Publishers* 2013
Text © Rachel Allen, 2013
Photographs © Tara Fisher, 2013

13 12 11 10 9 8 7 6 5 4 3 2 1

A catalogue record for this book is available from the British Library.

ISBN: 978-0-00-746237-7

Design: Louise Evans, www.gradedesign.com
Food Stylist: Joss Herd
Props Stylist: Liz Belton

Colour reproduction by FMG
Printed and bound in Italy by L.E.G.O. SpA